Please return / renew this item by the last date shown above
Dychwelwch / Adnewyddwch erbyn y dyddiad olaf y nodir yma

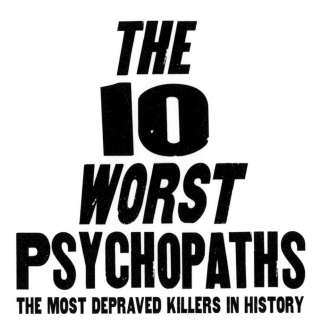

THE 10 WORST WORST PSYCHOPATHS

THE MOST DEPRAVED KILLERS IN HISTORY

VICTOR MCQUEEN

ARCTURUS

ARCTURUS

This edition published in 2016 by Arcturus Publishing Limited
26/27 Bickels Yard, 151–153 Bermondsey Street,
London SE1 3HA

ISBN: 978-1-78428-238-7
DA004675UK

Printed in China

CONTENTS

CONTENTS CONTINUED

INTRODUCTION

To the general public, the term 'psychopath' tends to be equated with violent and deranged criminality. Characters such as Norman Bates in Alfred Hitchock's celebrated 1960 film *Psycho* are far removed from real-life psychopaths, however. Bates was suffering from psychosis, which is a term associated with losing touch with reality. True psychopaths are aware of the difference between right and wrong: they simply choose to ignore anything that prevents them getting what they want. Real-life psychopaths are not mad but bad.

Although the basic concept of psychopathy has been recognized for centuries, it is only relatively recently that experts have agreed the characteristics that define the clinical psychopath. One of the pioneers of the modern research effort was Dr Robert Hare, who developed the Psychopathy Check List Revised (PCL-R) in an attempt to describe the degree of psychopathy an individual displays. The clusters of personality traits and socially deviant behaviours outlined in the checklist are separated into four types: interpersonal, affective, lifestyle and antisocial. Each trait and type is recorded by the expert in order to arrive at an overall score on the psychopathy scale.

Different institutions have their own scales and score weightings, but almost all look at a broadly similar combination of personality traits in order to reach a 'score' of psychopathy. This score is used to determine such factors as how best to treat the individual, and whether it is safe to allow the individual to live freely in society.

The most significant traits that appear in psychopathy tests are glibness, superficial charm, a grandiose sense of self, deceit, manipulation, a lack of remorse or empathy, thrill-seeking, impulsivity, criminal versatility and a lack of realistic life goals. Often psychopathic individuals will display early childhood behaviour problems; they are frequently in trouble with the law from a young age. They usually have poor or highly dysfunctional relationships with their parents and siblings.

Not all psychopaths score highly in all areas, and it is important to stress that not all psychopaths are necessarily violent. Indeed, one of the most troubling truths about psychopaths is that they appear in all walks of life, and often pass largely unnoticed by the majority of us. They may even be highly successful in their chosen field. Studies suggest that 'high-flyers' in the business world tend to score more highly than average on the psychopath scale, for example. Politics is another field in which psychopaths tend to flourish.

This book looks at some of history's most notorious and infamous psychopaths, and seeks to show how their life stories illustrate the classic psychopathic personality traits. We will look not only at serial killers but also at others who have brought mayhem, betrayal, death and destruction to a world that failed to recognize them for the dangerous individuals they were. Though all morally despicable, many of these individuals were charming, popular and charismatic. This is part of our enduring fascination with psychopaths: they are capable of extraordinary, inhuman acts; yet they appear on the surface to be entirely 'normal'. It is only once you know what to look for that the psychopathy beneath the cunning mask becomes obvious. For many, that moment of realization comes too late. Read on, and before long you will be able to recognize that you are working with, living next door to, or even related to a psychopath. None of them, hopefully, will score as highly on the psychopath scale as the individuals featured in this book. This is a collection of the very worst psychopaths from across the world, and from the very earliest times to the modern day.

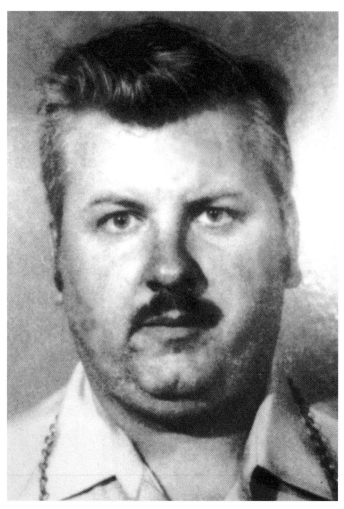

John Wayne Gacy

CHAPTER ONE
JOHN WAYNE GACY

In December 1978, John Wayne Gacy's lawyers filed a suit against the Des Plaines police, alleging that their constant harassment was making him unwell. Certainly, the close police surveillance of his house and movements seemed to be taking their toll on his physical appearance. He was unshaven and exhausted – and appeared to be constantly agitated. He had started drinking heavily. On the evening of 20 December, he drove over to his lawyer's office and asked for a stiff drink as soon as he walked in the door. He was there to discuss the progress of his lawsuit, but instead he launched into a long and rambling confession. He had killed people, he said. Lots of people. He reckoned about 30 'give or take a few'. Then he passed out in his lawyer's office chair.

The next day police raided his house at 8213 Summerdale in Norwood Park Township, Illinois. In the crawl space of his home they found putrefied human remains. In total, 26 bodies were wedged in the cramped space, with a further body buried under the concrete floor of his garage, another beneath the joists of his dining room floor and a final body in a pit in his back garden. He confessed to throwing four more bodies into the Des Plaines River.

Neighbours, friends and relatives of Gacy were horrified – and incredulous. He was a well-liked man in the local community, who often did charity work, frequently dressed as a clown. A successful businessman, he was active in Democratic Party politics and even met with First Lady Rosalynn Carter. How could a man like this be the killer of so many innocent young men? The answer came when psychiatrists assessed Gacy just before his trial on 33 counts of first-degree murder. John Wayne Gacy's score on the Psychopath Test checklist used by psychiatrists was one of the highest ever seen. The 'Killer Clown' was an almost perfect example of a psychopath.

A brutal father

John Wayne Gacy Junior was born in Chicago, Illinois, on 17 March 1942. The second of three children, he was of Polish and Danish extraction. Though John Wayne deeply admired his father the feeling was not reciprocated, and John Stanley Gacy was often physically and emotionally abusive to the boy. A chronic alcoholic, he was also violent towards his wife and John Wayne's two sisters. In later conversations with psychologists, John Wayne Gacy described one of his earliest memories as being beaten with a leather belt by his father. On one occasion he was struck so hard on the head with a broomstick that he was rendered unconscious.

Of the three children, it was John who took the brunt of the punishment, being described by his father as 'dumb' and mocked for his lack of physical fitness. His mother tried to protect him and as a result John Stanley became even more contemptuous of the boy, calling him a 'sissy Mama's boy' and remarking that he would probably 'grow up queer'.

From a very young age, Gacy showed a precocious interest in sex. He and another boy were caught molesting a girl at school when he was just seven years old. He was punished, as per usual, with a beating from his father. Later on, when Gacy began to be abused by one of his father's friends, he was too scared to tell anyone in case he was beaten again. He became withdrawn and sullen, which added to his sense of isolation at school. There he was bullied for being overweight and because he could not compete in sporting activities due to a congenital heart condition. Between the ages of 14 and 18, John Wayne Gacy spent over a year in hospital due to repeated blackouts. He fell behind with his grades. This caused more conflict with his tyrannical father, who felt his son needed toughening up. Gacy recalled how his father used to take the distributor cap off his car so he couldn't use it without permission. That kind of powerlessness is frustrating to most individuals, but in the psychopath it becomes a burning injustice that sooner or later tends to erupt into violence.

Respectable lifestyle

Gacy became fascinated with death after a brief stint working as a mortuary attendant. He later described how he climbed into the coffin of a deceased teenage male and caressed the body. The seeds of his later sex crimes were clearly evident, but for a long period John Wayne Gacy appeared to have turned his life around. He enrolled in Northwestern Business College despite failing to graduate from high school, and managed to find a position as a salesman at the Nunn-Bush Shoe Company.

He was soon transferred to Springfield, Illinois, and promoted to department manager. He met and married a co-worker, Marlynn Myers. In 1966 his father-in-law offered him the opportunity to manage three Kentucky Fried Chicken restaurants he owned in Waterloo, Iowa. The couple moved there and had two children, Michael and Christine. Even John Wayne's father was forced to admit to his son that he had been wrong about him: John

Wayne Gacy was by now a well-respected businessman, loving husband and father, and a major contributor to local charitable organizations.

In fact, beneath the skilfully created veneer, Gacy was leading a life of deviant sexual promiscuity behind his wife's back. He regularly hired prostitutes of both sexes, and opened a 'club' in the basement of his home where he invited employees to drink alcohol, take drugs and play pool.

Only young males were invited back, and they were regularly propositioned for sex. At first when they refused Gacy would just laugh it off as though he'd been making a joke. Later on such advances would become deadly serious, however.

It all started to unravel in August 1967. Gacy began to commit sexual offences against teenage boys, luring them back to his house by promising to show them pornographic videos, or claiming he was partaking in homosexual experiments for 'scientific research'. He was arrested in 1968 after one boy told his father, who contacted the police. Gacy reacted with the classic flat denial and protestation of innocence that characterizes the psychopath. He volunteered to take a polygraph test, which proved inconclusive. Polygraphs generally work on individuals who react to the stress of guilt and shame, and since psychopaths rarely feel these emotions they often pass 'lie detector' tests with flying colours.

Appearance matters far more to the psychopath than the mere technicality of their guilt or innocence. The lengths that Gacy would go to in order to preserve his veneer of respectability are evident in his next move. He paid one of his young employees $300 to beat up his victim, in order to intimidate the boy into dropping the charges. The employee, Russell Schroeder, attacked the young victim by spraying mace into his eyes and beating him up. The victim immediately reported the attack to police, and Schroeder admitted the crime when later arrested. He implicated Gacy in his confession, stating that it was Gacy who supplied the mace used in the attack.

Despite this damning testimony Gacy still chose to plead not guilty at trial, claiming his victim had consented to sex and admitting to only one count of sodomy. The jury found against him and he was sentenced to ten years in jail. His wife immediately filed for divorce, and Gacy never saw her or his children again. A psychiatric report on him diagnosed him with antisocial personality disorder and concluded he was always likely to offend, and was probably not treatable.

Free to attack again

Despite this assessment, Gacy was granted parole just 18 months into his ten-year sentence. He maintained to his friends that he was entirely innocent of all the crimes and he was guilty only of a lapse of judgement. Most stood by him – though by now his father had passed away. He moved back in with his mother in Chicago and took a job as a cook in a local restaurant. Within eight months he had been charged with sexually assaulting a teenage boy, and had the Iowa Parole Board been aware of this he would have been returned to prison. In the event, the boy failed to testify at court and the charges were dropped. Gacy remained free, and with financial help from his mother bought a house at 8213 West Summerdale Avenue in Cook County in 1971. It would later become infamous throughout the world as 'The House of Horror'.

Gacy remarried, and his new wife Carole Hoff moved in to the home shortly afterwards. A week before his wedding to the divorcee, Gacy was again arrested and charged with battery after a complaint from a young man. The victim claimed that Gacy had impersonated a police officer, flashing a sheriff's badge at him before forcing him to perform oral sex. Psychopaths are the ultimate impersonators as they learn from an early age to mimic the behaviour of those around them – pretence is second nature to them. The charges were dropped when the complainant allegedly attempted to blackmail Gacy, though that may well be a story that Gacy himself concocted.

Gacy decided to start his own construction business – Painting, Decorating and Maintenance, or PDM. It is a little-known fact that psychopaths generally make excellent business leaders, thanks to their confidence, expert communication skills and lack of social inhibitions. A recent study of top business leaders found that around 3 per cent of them scored highly on the psychopath scale, as opposed to around 1 per cent in the general population. So it should come as no surprise to learn that Gacy's PDM company did extremely well, and by 1978 had an annual turnover of some \$200,000.

The success emboldened Gacy and he revelled in his power as a boss. He raped a young male employee while on a business trip to Florida, and was later beaten up by the man in retaliation. That incident he explained away to his wife as a disagreement about wages, and to the community at large, Gacy appeared to be a pillar of the community. He was appointed director of the annual Polish Constitution Day Parade, and joined the local Moose Club. There he volunteered as a 'Jolly Joker' clown, regularly entertaining hospitalized children with his 'Pogo the Clown' act. He often didn't bother to change out of his clown outfit before retiring to the Good Luck Lounge, where he was a regular at the bar.

First murder

Beneath the thin veneer of respectability, however, lay a repressed sexual desire that was soon to lead to him discovering what he described as 'the ultimate thrill':

murder. He later claimed that his first victim, 15-year-old Timothy Jack McCoy, died as the result of an accident. According to Gacy, the boy had entered his bedroom carrying a knife in from the kitchen, where he was preparing breakfast. Gacy awoke, saw the knife, and assumed he was being attacked. He ended up killing the boy in what he thought at the time was self-defence.

It sounds like a lie. We'll never know, but it is likely that the boy tried to resist Gacy's advances and was stabbed repeatedly in the chest as a result. Gacy admitted to having an orgasm as he drove the knife into the boy, and if he were merely fighting off an attacker he would have been terrified rather than sexually excited. Psychopaths are pathological liars, even to themselves, so this may be the lie that Gacy told himself in order to explain his transition from respected businessman to pitiless serial killer.

Whatever the truth of the matter, Timothy's body was the first of many placed in the crawl space at his home in West Summerdale Avenue. When the corpse later started to decompose he covered it with a layer of concrete.

Gacy's next victim remains unidentified to this day. The killer himself estimated the victim to be aged between 14 and 18 when he strangled him in January 1974. Immediately after killing him, Gacy hid his body in a closet at his home, but fluid started leaking from the corpse's mouth and nose, so he buried him in his garden. In future murders

Gacy would stuff rags or underwear into the victims' mouths in order to prevent such fluid leaks, which he complained had stained his carpet.

Handcuffs and wrestling

Business at PDM was brisk and Gacy was working 16-hour days in order to keep up with orders. The frantic work schedule gave him the perfect excuse of working late to explain his extended absences from the home. Throughout 1975, Gacy regularly cruised for sex with young males, either by approaching men in local gay hang-outs or by propositioning his own workforce. His employees were largely young, physically fit young men fresh out of high school and desperate to impress their boss. For a psychopath, it was the perfect scenario. One such youngster was Anthony Antonucci, who had been working at PDM for only a couple of months when Gacy turned up at his home address. He used the pretence of checking on Anthony's health to gain access – Antonucci had injured his foot at work the day prior. Once inside Antonucci's home, Gacy wrestled him to the floor and handcuffed his hands behind his back. Fortunately for the young man, Gacy had left one cuff slightly loose, and Antonucci managed to free himself. Antonucci was a member of his high school wrestling team, and his would-be assailant suddenly found the tables turned: the young man wrestled Gacy to the floor and handcuffed him.

Gacy was released after promising to leave the house, and he tried to pass the incident off as horseplay. Antonucci did not report the matter to police. It left Gacy free to perform the same handcuff trick more successfully on a number of other victims. The first to die as a result was 17-year-old John Butkovitch, another PDM employee. He was lured to Gacy's home, ostensibly to settle a dispute about his wages. Gacy's wife and stepchildren were away visiting relatives, which gave the killer a rare opportunity to operate in safety.

Butkovitch was handcuffed, then strangled to death and buried under the concrete floor of Gacy's garage. It was extremely risky for Gacy to kill someone directly linked to him so soon after his failed attempt to handcuff another employee, but somehow he managed to get away with it. When he was interviewed by police on the matter, he appeared composed and helpful. He even assisted with the search for the missing boy. Butkovitch's parents rang the police more than 100 times to try to persuade them to take a longer look at John Wayne Gacy, who they were convinced knew something about their missing child, but no further action was taken.

Divorce – and a new wave of attacks

Gacy avoided any consequences for the murders thus far, but his lifestyle was taking its toll in other areas. The long hours away from home and his fondness for bringing teenage boys back to his garage led to tension in his marriage with Carole. When she found his collection of hardcore gay pornography, matters came to a head, and she divorced him in October 1975. She finally left the West Summerdale Avenue address in February 1976. Less than two months later, the newly single John Wayne Gacy killed again. His new victim was another young man, an 18-year-old named Darrell Sampson. Just five weeks later, 15-year-old Randall Reffett vanished while walking home from Senn High School. Within a few hours another boy went missing, too – this time it was 14-year-old Samuel Stapleton, on his way back from his sister's apartment. In a spate of murderous rage perhaps triggered by his divorce, Gacy had killed three times in just a few weeks.

This began a pattern that is common once a psychopath begins to feel confident in his ability to kill: the frequency of the murders increases and the crimes become more daring. In Gacy's case, he killed at least three more boys and young men throughout June and August, burying all of them in the crawl space at his home. He may have killed as many as four others during the same period – not all of the human remains recovered could be identified or given a precise time of death.

The period of slaughter was put on hold only when Gacy targeted an ex-Army youth, David Cram, who despite being handcuffed managed to lay Gacy out with a kick to the face. Cram was another PDM employee, and had been invited to live with Gacy before being attacked. He freed himself from the handcuffs, left the house and the employ of PDM, but did not report the incident to the police. So once again Gacy escaped arrest – and continued to kill.

Murders became a grim routine throughout the rest of 1976. All the victims were young men, either lured from the streets, cafés and bars of the locality or unfortunate enough to look for work at PDM. Concerned parents of the missing youths sometimes contacted Gacy to ask if he had any information. The parents of 17-year-old Gregory Godzik were told that he had left a message on Gacy's answerphone saying he had run away from home. In fact Gacy had murdered him, but his psychopathic mind could not resist toying with the grieving relatives. When they asked him to play them the message in question, Gacy told them he had erased it.

Like many psychopaths, Gacy kept 'trophies' from many of his victims, so he could relive the moment when he snuffed out their lives. He was particularly fond of 19-year-old John Szyc's ring, which bore his initials. It was later found in Gacy's bedroom. Szyc's body was with so many of the others in the crawl space.

But Gacy made a mistake in selling Szyc's car to another

PDM employee by the name of Michael Rossi. In August of 1977, Rossi was arrested for stealing gasoline from a garage while driving the car. The trail led back to John Wayne Gacy's address, where the car was still registered, and inevitably the police were soon knocking on the door of 8213 West Summerdale Avenue. Gacy explained that Szyc had sold the car to him before skipping town. The police had no reason to pursue the matter further, but Gacy was now on their radar in relation to the case.

A new outrage – torture

As so often is the case with psychopaths, this brush with the law did nothing to make Gacy nervous about continuing his murderous activities. He continued to kill the young men he lured back to his home, and by December 1977 he had progressed to forcing victims into his car at gunpoint. Robert Donnelly was approached in such a fashion at a Chicago bus stop and taken back to Gacy's home. Until this point Gacy had suffocated or strangled his victims, gaining sexual satisfaction from the murder itself.

The thrill of killing had lost its edge after being repeated so many times, however, and now Gacy needed to torture his victims in order to stimulate himself. He inflicted so much pain on Donnelly that the victim begged Gacy to kill him in order to end it. Gacy replied, with the psychopath's characteristic lack of empathy, that he was 'getting round to it'.

Eventually, however, he made the inexplicable decision to release his victim. The battered and bloody Donnelly went straight to the police, who immediately investigated. Incredibly, Gacy managed to brazen the matter out by claiming he had been engaging in consensual sado-masochistic sex with his victim. The police believed the respectable businessman rather than the kid from the streets, and no further action was taken.

Fatal mistake

One more victim found his way into Gacy's crawl space: 19-year-old William Kindred was murdered in February 1978. The crawl space was already packed with bodies and Gacy realized he would have to find somewhere else to dump his bodies. He chose Lincoln Park for his next victim. This would prove to be the mistake that would ultimately cost him his life.

The man he dumped there, 26-year-old Jeffrey Rignall, was unconscious but not dead. He had been chloroformed, raped, beaten and tortured with candle flames. Rignall managed to stagger back to his girlfriend's house and the police were called. However, all Rignall could give them was a description of his attacker, not the name, so they had little to go on. Later Rignall remembered his assailant's distinctive black Oldsmobile vehicle, and when he saw it driving along a nearby Expressway the following month he followed it back to 8213 West Summerdale.

This time there was to be no escape for Gacy. He was arrested and charged with battery. While still under that charge he nonetheless lured a 15-year-old boy called Robert Jerome Piest back to his home and murdered him. The fact he would do so even while under police scrutiny demonstrates just how reckless Gacy had become. The boy was enticed from a local pharmacy in broad daylight, and within sight and earshot of several witnesses. It was only a matter of time before police would link Gacy with the boy's disappearance – especially now that he was on their radar for a violent sexual assault against another young man. He was placed under intense surveillance and repeatedly questioned, until he finally cracked and confessed to his lawyer.

No humanity, no empathy

He pleaded not guilty by reason of insanity at his trial in February 1980. Doctors spent more than 300 hours examining him at the Menard Correctional Center before the case reached court, and found him legally sane and thus criminally responsible for his actions. The defence claimed he was a paranoid schizophrenic who suffered from multiple personality disorder, but the prosecution maintained he was a cunning psychopath who committed premeditated murder for sexual gratification.

As those who survived his brutal attacks gave their testimony in court, Gacy laughed and openly mocked them. The utterly heartless lack of compassion or remorse simply confirmed that the prosecution analysis was the correct one. The jury took less than two hours to find Gacy guilty on 33 charges of murder, and he was sentenced to death.

Gacy spent the next 14 years appealing his conviction. He read countless law books and tried every avenue to find a way to escape the death penalty. It was to no avail and he was executed on the evening of 9 May 1994. His final words were: 'Kiss my ass'.

Chicago police use a ground-penetrating radar to look for the bodies of more of Gacy's victims.

An engraving depicting the Harpe
brothers in their frontiersmen clothes.

CHAPTER 2

THE HARPE BROTHERS

The American 'Wild West' had more than its fair share of violent criminals, and many murderous gunslingers have passed into folklore as freedom-loving anti-heroes. Even by the standards of 18th-century frontier America, however, Micajah 'Big' Harpe and his brother Wiley 'Little' Harpe were out of the ordinary: feared and despised in equal measure. Not for them the Hollywood treatment given to Jesse James or Billy the Kid; today, if they are remembered at all, it is as psychopathic killers of the most reviled kind. Many historians argue, in fact, that they were America's first true serial killers, motivated not by financial gain but by sexual sadism.

Exactly when and where they were born we do not know for sure. The most reliable account of their lives was written by James Hall, a judge in Shawneetown, in his 1828 book *Letters From The West*. Hall skips the early part of their lives, however, and focuses on the later years when they were 'spreading death and terror wherever they went'. Most sources suggest they were born between 1768 and 1770, and grew up in North Carolina before moving to Virginia with their parents to seek work on a slave plantation as overseers. Though widely described as brothers, some sources claim they were in fact cousins. They may have emigrated from Scotland at an early age; certainly most reports mention some kind of Scottish ancestry, with many mentioning that their parents were loyal to the British crown.

In the British militia

This background probably influenced the Harpes to fight for the British in the American Revolution. Although no definite record of their involvement has been handed down to us, several separate reports by reliable eyewitnesses mention the Harpes by name. One captain claimed that the brothers were involved in the kidnap and gang-rape of teenage girls in North Carolina. Militias and gangs at the time often took advantage of the mayhem of war to raid settlements and rob, rape and destroy whomever and whatever they found. Other eyewitnesses place the Harpe brothers in the ranks of British militia at several key battles during the war. These accounts may be the result of historical embellishment, however, as the Harpe brothers would have been very young at this date – if their recorded birth dates are accurate. It is possible that the actions of the Harpes' older relatives have been mixed in with the story of the two notorious brothers.

Following the British defeats at the Battle of Kings Mountain in 1780 and Yorktown in 1781, they were said to have fled from North Carolina to Tennessee villages beyond the Appalachian Mountains and then regrouped with Native American tribes there. Their property and possessions were seized by the Patriots, who were bent on driving 'Tory' sympathizers from the region. A burning sense of injustice raged within Micajah and his younger brother. The Creek and Cherokee Native Americans shaped the Harpe Brothers' hatred of the 'white settler' frontiersmen who had defeated the British crown. With a common cause to unite them, the Harpes and renegade Native American warriors launched fierce attacks against any pioneers who journeyed into their lands. They survived by stealing and hunting until Major James Ore launched a fierce counter-attack on the Native American settlement of Nickajack, forcing the Harpes to flee to a cabin near the Holston River, 13 kilometres outside of Knoxville.

For a short period, they appear to have settled down to a harsh domestic life that many frontiersmen at the time would have recognized as entirely normal. Little Harpe married Sarah 'Sally' Rice, the daughter of a Knoxville minister, in the summer of 1797. Micajah married Susanna Roberts a couple of months later, though a 'Betsy Roberts' is also recorded as staying at the cabin. Some reports suggest that the Harpe brothers shared the three women sexually without regard as to who was married to whom. This was very much the Wild West, where social and moral norms had not yet been established – survival was the key priority. The Harpes probably raised little attention in their Beaver Creek home, save for their distaste for wearing hats. Little Harpe had a shock of flaming red hair, and Big Harpe's mop was said to be dark and curly, some say as a result of an African American slave bloodline. He was a powerful man, over six foot tall, and carried a large tomahawk with him wherever he went. There is no confirmation that any crimes took place during this period, though several sources suggest that the Harpes routinely murdered the children born to them at the cabin.

Outlaws

What ended the period of relative peace was Big Harpe's love of risk-taking. It's a common trait in psychopaths, who are drawn to danger like a moth to a flame. The brothers bet their entire farm on a single horse race, and lost – some say they literally lost their shirts, too. They had no option but to take off into the forests of the nearby Cumberland Mountains, and the caves and thickets there would remain their home for the rest of their days. To survive they would rely on robbery, and one of their first victims was the Methodist preacher Reverend William Lambuth, accosted as he rode through the woods in 1797. He was divested of all his valuables, but escaped with his life – rare among those who encountered the Harpes. As the two brothers disappeared back into the forest with Lambuth's valuables, Big Harpe turned to bellow: 'We are the Harpes!' It is a telling insight into the mind of the man: he was not interested in disguising his identity, as most highwaymen and robbers would be. Instead he made a point of declaring exactly who he was, as if proud of his crime. This is exactly the sort of grandiose showmanship that distinguishes the psychopath from the common criminal.

Naturally, the ostentatious sneering of the Harpes drew the attention of the local community. A man named Edward Tiel put together a posse of men to track down the bandits after they stole a number of his horses. The Harpes made no effort to hide and were easily caught. While being marched back to Knoxville to face trial, however, the brothers somehow managed to quietly slip back into the woods. How they accomplished this feat of escapology is not clear, but it was to cost the local community dear. Up until this point the Harpes had been a nuisance, stealing valuable livestock and burning down barns. This latter trademark act is another common characteristic of psychopaths, who frequently commit acts of arson before turning to acts of murder. That's exactly how it panned out in the story of the fugitive Harpe brothers, who embarked on a killing spree of unparalleled barbarism in the years that followed.

'Hyper-violence'

A close encounter with law enforcement does not strike fear or caution into the psychopathic mind, but rather gives it a 'high' and enforces the egotistical belief in invincibility. This can be seen in the actions of the Harpe brothers, who rather than laying low chose immediately to visit a bar a few kilometres west of Knoxville. It appears they were not intending to celebrate their escape, but rather to track down the man they believed had informed the posse of their location in the woods. When they found the unfortunate man, they hauled him out of the bar; his body was found several days later in the Holston River. He had been ripped open and his body filled with stones. The grisly mutilation of the body would become a trademark of Harpe brothers' murders. It is a type of 'hyper-violence' that extends beyond the kind of injury required to kill, as if the murderer must exceed even the limit of death. The revulsion most human beings feel when in the presence of a dead body is absent in the psychopath:

a corpse is a lump of meat and nothing more.

The Harpes travelled east to the Cumberland Gap, and it seems the dam of their bloodlust had by now broken. They killed anyone they met who might have something they needed or wanted. A peddler named Peyton was the first victim on their bloody Kentucky journey. He was killed for his horse and goods. Two travellers from Maryland called Paca and Bates were the next to encounter the Harpes on the Wilderness Road: both were slain. Bates died instantly from a gunshot to the back, Paca tried to stagger away with a gunshot wound of his own but had his head cleaved in two by Big Harpe's tomahawk. Then a day or two later a young man named Langford was murdered after being foolish enough to offer to pay for the fugitives' food and lodgings. They noticed he was in possession of a large number of silver coins, and his fate was sealed.

Arrested and jailed

The victims' bodies were disposed of with a casual disregard, and were soon discovered by passing drovers. The distinctive Harpe brothers were easily identified as the likely culprits and a posse set off in pursuit of them. The Harpes and their three womenfolk were arrested for the second time on Christmas Day in 1799 and remanded in prison at Danville, Kentucky. By this time all three of the women were pregnant.

The Harpe brothers had no qualms about leaving them behind in prison as they plotted their own escape. Emotional attachments of any kind are seen by psychopaths as weaknesses.

The breakout took place on 16 March 1800. Exactly how the Harpes executed it is again lost in the mists of time, but security in jails during this period was frequently poor. Keys left close to locks, jail staff falling asleep or getting drunk, corruption – all of these were common-place. Records show that the jail invested in a bolt and horse-locks for the men's feet and a heavy new lock for the front door. But the same records show that the jail spent a further 12 shillings on repairs to the hewn log structure of the jailhouse due to the damage caused by the Harpes in their escape.

And what is known for sure is that within a couple of weeks of the brothers' escape, two further men lay dead at their hands. On 10 April they escalated their murderous activity by killing a 13-year-old boy, the son of Colonel Daniel Trabue, a leading former Revolutionary soldier. The boy's pet dog led the posse to his body, which had been chopped into pieces and stuffed down a sinkhole. Traube joined the pursuing posse, bent on revenge, but the trail went cold and the Harpe brothers simply moved on out, to another part of the vast expanse of uninhabited land.

The three 'wives' still held in prison in Danville all

gave birth to healthy children. After a mistrial, they were all released and given a horse to allow them to return home, after being warned to stay clear of the Harpe brothers. However, in what would appear to be some kind of early example of Stockholm syndrome, or capture-bonding, they traded the horse for a canoe and set off down the Green River to rejoin the brutal brothers at an agreed rendezvous. The location in question was on the banks of the mighty Ohio River, and was feared by all but the most hardened of outlaws.

The Harpes and their wives hunkered down in the massive complex of limestone cliff passages known as Cave-in-Rock in southern Illinois. It was a spot popular with riverboat pirates, who ambushed and robbed the passing flatboats. The pirates were fellow outlaws but of the common-or-garden variety, and they soon evicted the new tenants after the Harpes supposedly murdered a riverboat passenger purely for entertainment. The story goes that they lashed the man naked onto a horse, then blindfolded both man and horse and drove the horse off a cliff 30 metres high. Even the bloodthirsty pirates recognized there was something more than mere criminality at work in the psyche of the brothers: this was sadism, driven by a psychopathic lack of empathy for other human beings. In truth, the story about the blindfolded horse and rider crops up in several stories about the Wild West and may have become attached to the Harpe brothers only after their deaths. Even if this is the case, however, the reason such stories become associated with the Harpes is because of the brothers' reputation for sadistic violence. That reputation was unquestionably deserved, as their next well-documented murder demonstrates.

The brothers and their wives moved through Tennessee, leaving a trail of blood wherever they went. They knew they were being pursued, and with a $300 bounty on their heads they could afford to trust no one. The brothers changed their appearance and split up from their wives, posing as Methodist preachers. They made their way to the home of Moses Stegall, who allegedly owed them money. Stegall wasn't home but his wife was, and she repaid them the sum in full – one dollar – and offered them a bed for the night. The room they slept in was one shared with a guest of the Stegalls, Major William Love. Big Harpe didn't care for the way he snored, so he smashed a tomahawk through his skull to silence him. Even a trivial matter can be fatal when you are in the company of a psychopath.

The following morning they murdered the Stegalls' four-month-old baby because its cries were delaying their mother from making them breakfast. When Mrs Stegall discovered the baby lying in a pool of blood with its throat cut she began to scream, and the Harpe brothers used the same knife to cut her throat, too. They then set fire to the family's cabin and watched it burn. When two neighbours came across the blaze, the Harpe brothers accused them of setting the fire, and arrested them. They were hoping to use them as bait to ambush Justice of the Peace Squire Silas McBee, towards whom they bore a grudge. McBee dodged the ambush, however, so the Harpes simply executed their two prisoners by shooting them both in the head. Some reports suggest that Big Harpe actually cleaved one of the men's head in two with his tomahawk. Another version of the story states that the Harpe brothers took the identities of their two victims and claimed they had arrested the notorious Harpe brothers, in order to confuse the lawmen on their tail. They escaped on horseback, pursued by a posse of seven local men.

The posse caught up with the Harpes the next day, and the two brothers rode off in different directions in order to maximize their chances of escape. The main posse rode after Big Harpe, as he was considered the more dangerous of the two. Four men fired at Big Harpe but only one bullet hit him as he galloped away. Big Harpe's steed was Major Love's horse, a large and powerful beast, and only one of the pursuing men had a horse quick enough to keep up. John Lieper closed the gap and fired his rifle, but missed. Harpe returned fire and also missed. Lieper's second shot tore through Big Harpe's backbone, wounding him severely. After about another kilometre, Harpe's tomahawk slipped from his hand to the earth and he himself slumped forward in his saddle. He was pulled down and given a drink of water and a chance to pray. Big Harpe waived the opportunity to repent, but he did admit to having committed a total of 20 murders.

Harpe's Head

Moses Stegall, whose wife and child Big Harpe had killed, was part of the posse and was given the opportunity to exact justice, Wild West style. He sawed off Big Harpe's head with his own butcher's knife. Harpe's last words were reported as: 'You're a God-damned rough butcher, but cut on and be damned.' Some accounts state Stegall set to work while Harpe was still alive, others maintain he shot the man through the heart first. Either way, the head was taken back to the crossroads near Stegall's cabin and displayed there as a warning to other outlaws. The intersection became known as Harpe's Head. Stegall himself was gunned down less than a year later after helping another outlaw kidnap a young woman, so any pleasure he gained from his act of vengeance was short-lived. In the Wild West almost everything and everyone was short-lived.

Little Harpe fared little better than Big Harpe. Although he managed to evade capture for several years, and escape from captivity twice more, his luck ran out in January

1804 when he was tried and convicted of murder. He was hanged in Greenville, Mississippi, and his head was then cut off and placed on a stake along the Natchez Road. The Harpe reign of terror was finally at an end, leaving at least 25 people dead. Many put the figure at over 50, and the pair are often referred to as America's first true serial killers.

Unlike most serial killers, however, they murdered almost entirely at random, butchering whomever they happened to encounter, regardless of race, age or gender. They took full advantage of the fact that America's frontier country was poorly policed and largely lawless, as well as being sparsely populated – so that capture was less likely. In the end, however, their crimes were so despicable that the citizens of those lands, despite being well used to a harsh life and widespread violence, took matters into their own hands and tracked them down. When finally caught, both of the brothers suffered justice Wild West style – swift and brutal.

The three Harpe wives were treated far more mercifully, and eventually were considered to be just three more victims of the Harpe brothers' psychotic mind-control. They were released into society and all three remarried and went on to lead quiet and respectable lives.

Richard Kuklinski enters court for his trial in 1988.

CHAPTER 3

RICHARD 'THE ICEMAN' KUKLINSKI

Organized crime gangs such as the Mafia are notorious for their violence and brutal intolerance of disloyalty. However, a recent study found that, contrary to expectation, most members of the Mafia are not, in fact, psychopathic. They kill and maim in order to keep a tight control over their operations: to the Mafia dons, murder is 'just business'. For the most part the Mafia is careful not to target 'civilians'; its members fight instead among themselves. This discrimination and control is not a trait that tends to be found in the psychopathic mindset, where violence is often exhibited with a casual disdain for the lives of others.

The Mafia does sometimes, however, employ the services of psychopaths in order to carry out the bloody deeds that its business demands. One of the most notorious examples is Richard Kuklinski, a contract killer who became known as 'The Iceman'.

A hated father

Kuklinski was born in New Jersey in April 1935. His father, a brakeman on the railroad, was a Polish immigrant with a violent temper, and quite possibly a psychopath himself. He beat his children savagely from an early age, as well as beating his Irish Roman Catholic wife. On one occasion he attacked his eldest son, Florian, so ferociously that the boy died from his injuries. The family had to cover up the murder by claiming that Florian fell down the stairs.

After his elder brother's death, Richard was the most regularly beaten of the remaining three children. His mother would sometimes also beat him with broom handles and other household items. Richard vented his frustration and inner pain by torturing and killing cats and other small animals – a behaviour pattern seen time and time again in diagnosed psychopaths. Kuklinski experimented with ever more cruel ways to inflict pain on living creatures: on one occasion he tied two cats' tails together and threw them over a telephone wire to watch them claw one another to death.

There is a debate over whether psychopaths are born or created, whether the cause is nature or nurture. In the case of Kuklinski it seems clear that he inherited his cruel and sadistic temperament from his father – either through blood or through the monstrous abuse that the young

Richard suffered at his father's hands. 'I hated my father,' Kuklinski later said. 'If I could have, I would probably have killed him. Probably would have felt good about it, too ... He gave me this impersonal feeling I have when people die in front of me.' When his younger brother, Joseph, was convicted of raping and murdering a 12-year-old girl in 1970, Richard shrugged and remarked, 'We come from the same father.'

Kuklinski roamed the streets and pool halls of Jersey City in order to escape from the abuse at home. By the time he reached his teens he was known throughout the city as a pool shark who would explode with violence if angered. He later claimed that he committed his first murder at the age of just 14. The details of that case cannot be confirmed, but it is telling that Kuklinski described feeling 'empowered' by the incident. Almost all psychopaths share this desperate lust for power, and it is often because their childhood has left them feeling entirely helpless and robbed of free will. That is certainly what Richard Kuklinski's brutally violent upbringing left him feeling.

Manhattan murders

We only have Kuklinski's word for his earliest years of murder and mayhem, and most psychopaths are inveterate liars, so it is wise to take his testimony with a few large grains of salt. That said, much of what he later recounted did appear to tie in with police records of unsolved crimes committed at the time. According to Kuklinski, in the mid-1950s he began to travel to the West Side of Manhattan in search of people to murder. He did so purely to perfect the art of killing, and because slaughtering strangers gave him a thrill. It was always men that he stabbed, bludgeoned, strangled or shot to death – in public he often prided himself on never killing women, though that was almost certainly a lie, too. He stated that 'loud-mouthed' people reminded him of his father, and as a result he could become violent whenever he encountered such a person. One example was a teenager who insulted him in a bar: Kuklinski later found the young man drunk and sleeping in a car, and he burnt him alive in retaliation for the insult. Psychopaths have no sense of proportionality, and as far as Kuklinski was concerned the 'loudmouth' got what he deserved.

Kuklinski later justified his move into organized crime by saying that he realized he enjoyed murdering people and decided he might as well get paid for it rather than doing it for free. Some reports state that he first encountered the Gambino crime family while selling them pornographic videos at the film lab where he worked. Others claim that a Mafia enforcer was sent to recover a debt that Kuklinski owed, and the way that Kuklinski accepted his punishment-beating without resistance impressed the enforcer. Either way, the Gambinos noted that he was a physically intimidating man – 1.96 metres and weighing 135 kilograms – and his reputation for violence soon reached their ears. In order to test his loyalty they first gave him small jobs, but even these paid enough for him to abandon any thoughts of a legitimate career. He quit his regular job and began working full-time for the Mafia. In 1961, he married his wife, Barbara, and moved into a quiet and affluent neighbourhood in Dumont, New Jersey.

The normal routine of family life was often interrupted by Kuklinski suddenly leaving in order to 'take care of business'. Whenever he was called, no matter the time of day or night, he was ready and willing to do his bosses' bidding. He would sometimes leave the family home in the middle of a meal, or in the small hours of the morning. Such an existence suits the psychopathic mindset, which is impulsive and resistant to any kind of routine. Neighbours believed he was a successful businessman who was something of a workaholic. This was a façade that Kuklinski was keen to cultivate, and like most psychopaths he was a consummate showman and fraudster with a quick smile and breezy cheerful disposition.

At work, however, he was a very different character. The ability to compartmentalize different sides of a personality is not unique to psychopaths, but many of them do become masters of the art. This is illustrated in one episode of Kuklinski's life involving a minor debt he was owed by an associate. When the man explained he could not pay the debt, Kuklinski was at first understanding and reasonable. But later, at home, as he was wrapping his children's Christmas presents, he became more and more irate about the lack of repayment. He left the family home shortly after midnight and drove to New York in search of the man. When he found him, he shot him in the head and took the money he was owed (leaving behind a bundle of banknotes that he felt was not rightfully his). He then calmly drove back to the family home and continued wrapping his children's Christmas presents.

Mafia enforcer

Even among the battle-hardened ranks of the Mafia, Kuklinski was feared as a ruthless and hugely violent enforcer. He was no longer sent on the minor jobs of punishment beatings or 'warning visits'. Kuklinski was sent in when murder and torture were the victim's sentence. According to Kuklinski, his suitability for such a role was tested by gang *soldato* ('soldier') Roy DeMeo, who took him to a quiet city street, pointed out a man walking a dog and ordered Kuklinski to kill him. Although the man was a totally innocent and random stranger, Kuklinski had no hesitation in stepping out of the car and shooting him in the back of the head. He proved that he was up to the job – and that he was a true psychopath with absolutely no empathy for other human beings.

With practice, Kuklinski got better and better at the job he was asked to do. Initially he was surprised at the way a man's head exploded when blasted at close range by a shotgun ('like a pumpkin or something,' he later said). But though surprised, he was never nauseated or emotionally troubled by the hits he performed. 'To care is a weakness,' he later remarked. 'When you care you have baggage.'

He had no problem dismembering bodies with a butcher's knife, either. The smell sometimes 'annoyed' him, but he would overcome this bothersome detail by splashing cologne just under his nose. Even serial killer Jeffrey Dahmer was repulsed by dismembering bodies, and had to get drunk in order to do it, but for Kuklinski it was simply a routine part of his everyday work. As uncaring, clinical hitmen go, Kuklinski was a natural.

Gruesome experiments

For Kuklinski, half the fun of killing lay in thinking up novel methods to commit murder. He grew bored with simple shootings, and experimented with countless other ways to end the lives of his victims. On one occasion he wound down the window and asked a total stranger for directions. When the man leaned forward to offer help, Kuklinski shot him through the forehead with a crossbow. He explained later that he did this simply to see if a crossbow bolt fired at short range would kill a man. It did. Now and then Kuklinski left his guns, knives and tyre irons at home and simply beat a victim to death with his bare hands 'for the exercise'. The constant need for new and different experiences is a classic trait of the psychopath, and in Kuklinski we have one of the most barbaric examples of it.

He enjoyed the challenging hits the most. He fondly recalled one of his favourite assassinations, when he was tasked with killing a member of a rival crime syndicate who always had well-armed bodyguards around him. Kuklinski observed that the man frequented a particular club, and hatched a plan to kill him there without being detected. He put on a canary yellow sweater and platform heels and stepped onto the dance floor, mingling with the crowd until he was close to the victim. Then he pretended to stumble, and while doing so injected the man with cyanide. The poison was one of Kuklinski's favourite methods of murder.

The total number of people that Kuklinski killed is not known. He himself claimed that it was in excess of 200, but he couldn't give a precise figure because 'in order to count them you'd have to remember them'. Since Kuklinski was entirely uninterested in his victims, he wasn't troubled by memories of them, let alone bothered by any guilt or remorse. His only concern was how to get rid of the vast number of corpses he was responsible for. It was while experimenting with methods to achieve this that Kuklinski obtained his nickname of 'The Iceman'. Aware that pathologists could establish the time of a person's death by looking at the decay of their body, Kuklinski took to storing his victims in a freezer for weeks, months or even years. When the search for the missing victim was called off, he would thaw out the bodies before disposing of them. That way, a person killed a long time prior would appear to be freshly deceased. It was an incredibly cunning and cynical way to confuse crime scene investigators and increase his odds of getting away with his crimes. Other novel ways of disposing of bodies included placing the body in the boot of a car and then having it crushed in a junkyard. His favourite was simply placing a body in an oil drum and driving it a long way from anywhere before dumping it.

Undercover operation

The Iceman had few friends, and trusted no one. However, one person was at least close enough to him to act as a lure for a police sting operation. His name was Phil Solimene, and he agreed to introduce an undercover police officer to Kuklinski and vouch for the officer's cover story that he was a fellow hit man. The police taped the undercover officer talking to Kuklinski about how he might go about tackling a particularly problematic hit, and the Iceman couldn't resist explaining some of the techniques that he might use. It was enough for the authorities finally to arrest him, after an extensive secret operation that had gathered evidence against him for months.

Fortunately for the police, Kuklinski had started to get sloppy towards the end of his murderous career, and made several key mistakes. It's how psychopaths often come undone: they don't care for the humdrum details of covering up their crimes, and focus instead on the thrill and excitement of the next one.

Kuklinski's first key mistake was related to the murder of 37-year-old Gary Smith in Room 31 of the York Motel in North Bergen, New Jersey, in 1982. The Iceman's plan had been to inject the man with cyanide, but after he did so Smith took longer to die than Kuklinski had bargained for. Impatient, Kuklinski and his associate Daniel Deppner decided to finish him off by strangling him with the cord of a bedside lamp. The car that was meant to arrive to take away the body failed to show, so they simply stuffed the body under the mattress and remade the bed. Several people slept in the bed over the course of the next four days, and eventually patrons began to complain about the smell. When the body was found it was clear from the ligature marks on its neck that the victim had been murdered, and the police became involved. Had Kuklinski just left the victim in his bed and waited for the cyanide to take effect, the death might well been written off as having been caused by natural causes. But psychopaths are impatient and become bored easily.

They also have trust issues: Kuklinski's co-assassin in the Smith case, Daniel Deppner, was found murdered a few months later. He had been dumped close to a ranch where the police had observed that the Kuklinski family went riding. Deppner was the third associate of Kuklinski who had turned up dead, and the police began to join the dots. By now Kuklinski was working for himself, and without anyone ordering him around he felt he could do whatever he pleased. The result was that his work became dangerously casual. A body he had kept for two years in a freezer was dumped near a town park in Orangetown, New York, where it was clearly visible and thus easily discovered. Because of this, the ice crystals inside the body had not had a chance to thaw fully and the pathologist noted them. Since the body was found on a warm September day, the investigators deduced that it must have been stored in a freezer sometime prior to being dumped.

The net was closing in on Kuklinski. He agreed to take on the tricky hit that the undercover officer had spoken

COLOMBIA'S REIGN OF TERROR:

COCAINE KILLS

PART 4 OF WHY THE SMUGGLERS ARE WINNING — Starts on Page 7

DAILY◎NEWS

35¢   NEW YORK'S PICTURE NEWSPAPER®   Thursday, December 18, 1986

Nancy: They deceived Ron
Page 3

BURGER MURDER

N.J. man held in killings of 5 with gun & cyanide

Story on page 2

HASENFUS IS FREE

Nicaraguan President Daniel Ortega as he handed over gunrunner Eugene Hasenfus (left) to Sen. Christopher Dodd (right) in Managua yesterday. At far right is prisoner's wife, Sally. Hasenfus will arrive home today and may be summoned before congressional committees investigating the Contragate scandal. **Page 5**

The headline of the Daily News the day after Kuklinski's arrest in December 1986.

to him about, and the pair were secretly recorded exchanging the cyanide necessary for the operation. The police surrounded his house and arrested him on 17 December 1986. He was charged with five murder counts, as well as multiple counts of robbery, attempted murder and weapons violations. He was eventually convicted on five counts of murder and received consecutive sentences for the crimes, making him ineligible for parole until the age of 110.

Celebrity prisoner

While he languished in prison Kuklinski grandstanded to the media by granting several interviews in which he recounted his crimes in gruesome detail. American TV network HBO recorded three separate documentaries about him, in which he grinned and joked about his violent murders. He explained how he forced his victims to look him directly in the eye as he killed them because he wanted to see their expression at the exact moment they died. On many occasions, he told reporters, his clients had specifically requested that he make his victims suffer before they died. Naturally, Kuklinski was happy to oblige. He would take some victims into a remote rat-infested cave, tie them up and allow the rats to eat the victims alive. The slow and agonizing deaths were captured on a Super-8 camera, and the film reels sent to the client. 'There was a lot of screaming and yelling,' remarked a smirking Kuklinski. 'I did that quite a few times. Maybe too many times,' he said.

Far from being remorseful, he revelled in his barbarous reputation. 'I'm not looking for forgiveness and I'm not repenting,' he told one reporter. When asked whether he ever thought about the countless victims he killed he replied 'remembering them might make me sad. I don't wish to be sad. What's done is done.' There can be no more chilling example of the psychopath's complete lack of empathy than this: 'The Iceman' is truly a fitting nickname for Richard Kuklinski. He died, at the age of 70, on 5 March 2006.

Oskar Dirlewanger in his uniform.

CHAPTER 4

OSKAR DIRLEWANGER

The Nazi Party that led Germany into the Second World War had perhaps more psychopaths within it than any other political organization in history. It is difficult to pick out a single individual amid so many who were so cruel, but for a man who epitomizes the psychopathic mindset we need look no further than Oskar Dirlewanger. The SS officer is cited time and again by war historians as the very worst example of the inhumanity of the Nazi war machine. He is also an extreme example of what a psychopath is capable of, given the freedom and power to enact his darkest desires.

Dirlewanger was born on 26 September 1895 in Würzburg. He was the son of August and Pauline Herrlinger Dirlewanger, a middle-class couple living an affluent life in the Swabian region of Imperial Germany. His father was a lawyer and by all accounts Oskar was an intelligent child who in other circumstances might have followed in his father's footsteps into a respectable profession. He passed the Abitur test that allows German school leavers to pass into college, but then the outbreak of the First World War changed his life forever. Oskar signed up and fought with a bravery that was considered almost suicidal by his comrades-in-arms.

Here we have our first glimpse in Oskar's life of a classic psychopathic trait: the love of risk and danger. Most psychopaths believe they are invincible and almost immortal, and they therefore rarely experience fear. This quality can often seem admirable, particularly in times of war, and so it proved with Dirlewanger. He was rewarded for his efforts with both classes of Germany's illustrious military award, the Iron Cross.

Sex scandals

He continued to serve as a soldier in various brigades during the inter-war period, before finishing his education and becoming a professor of political science. Known for his extreme right-wing views and violent anti-Semitism, he was an early supporter of the Nazi Party, first joining it in 1923. Like many psychopaths he had problems with authority and was soon in trouble for insubordination. Despite this, he managed to use flattery to work his way up the ranks and get himself noticed as a dedicated party member. He may well have gone on to become a key aide to Hitler had he managed to keep out of trouble; but shortly afterwards the respected professor and war hero very seriously sabotaged his reputation with a sex scandal. He crashed a Nazi staff car while drunk, and was found to be in the company of a young girl who complained that he had sexually assaulted her. A police report described him as a mentally unstable, violent alcoholic who was often under the influence of mind-altering drugs. In 1934 he was kicked out of the Nazi Party and sent to prison for two years on a charge of molestation. He was released from the penitentiary at Ludwigsburg in October 1936 and placed on parole for three years. By then he had been stripped of his medical title and all military honours.

Psychopaths are often sexually promiscuous and drawn to taboo sexual encounters that offer them the promise of excitement. This was the case with Dirlewanger, who appears to have had a reputation for sexual perversion long before he was actually convicted of any crime. He never married, seemingly being incapable of forming lasting emotional bonds with adults. Like many psychopaths he preferred to have a series of short, intense relationships – and often forced himself sexually on those too vulnerable to resist him. Within months of being released from his first prison sentence he was back behind bars – this time at Welzheim, a concentration camp of a similar kind to those that would become notorious in the war years. Dirlewanger used his contacts with the top brass of the German military to gain his release in exchange for serving in a Nazi volunteer brigade in the Spanish Civil War. He was already showing the cunning and manipulative personality that is the hallmark of the psychopath.

When war with Britain was announced, Dirlewanger was desperate to rejoin the German military and was granted a commission as an SS officer. His reputation had not recovered, however, and he was refused command of a standard SS unit, being charged instead with turning a rag-tag militia of ex-poachers and other criminals into a military force. It was this band of armed convicts that formed the basis of SS Sonderkommando Dirlewanger, the SS unit that would soon hold the dubious distinction of having the worst record of atrocities in the whole of the Nazi war machine.

The ex-poachers were trained to hunt men instead of animals, and specialized initially in tracking down and murdering partisans in Poland. Anyone caught was shown no mercy, and Dirlewanger set an example to his troops by personally getting involved in the most barbarous acts of violence. The unit would regularly get drunk and go on the rampage in local villages, where innocent civilians were just as likely to be the targets of rape and torture as any resistance members.

No boundaries

After allegations of abuse, SS Judge Georg Konrad Morgen investigated Dirlewanger and described him as a 'terror to the entire population'. Dirlewanger would invite his friends around to witness his acts of barbarous torture as if it were a live entertainment show. On one occasion he had a female prisoner stripped and whipped, and then injected her with strychnine in order to watch her convulse to death on the floor.

Dirlewanger's period in Poland is also one source for the persistent rumour that the Nazis made soap from human flesh. Jewish women, in particular, were said to be a target of Dirlewanger's sadism and in Poland he found a plentiful supply. His persistent drunkenness and utter lack of discipline did not count against him in a land totally under the control of the German army. In saner times he would undoubtedly have faced court-martial, but the Nazi attitude was that Jews were subhuman and for a long period Dirlewanger was left to do as he pleased. For a psychopath, unfettered power is an ideal situation. Eventually, however, it leads to self-destruction, as there are simply no boundaries that a psychopath will not cross. In Poland, after several months, even Dirlewanger's fanatical fellow-Nazis began to be repulsed by the sadistic mayhem for which he was responsible.

Jews in the ghetto of Lublin in Poland where
Dirlewanger sought victims.

In 1942 Friedrich-Wilhelm Krüger, the SS chief in Poland, learnt of Dirlewanger's atrocities and determined to be rid of him. He described Dirlewanger's men as 'a bunch of criminals' and threatened to lock them up himself unless they were sent elsewhere. So the unit was moved on, beginning a pattern that would last throughout the war. Initially they were sent to Belarus, ostensibly to pacify the partisan fighters based there. Dirlewanger brought with him his trademark 'method': indiscriminate slaughter of the local population. His favourite trick was to round up the local men in a convenient barn, then set fire to it. Any who attempted to escape the fate of being burnt alive were mowed down with machine-gun fire. The young women were generally raped and tortured, before being shot. Civilians were often used as human shields to clear areas that had been mined. Conservative estimates of the number of people killed by Dirlewanger's death squads are in the region of 30,000. Others suggest the number could be triple or even quadruple that.

Unrestricted power

By now Dirlewanger's Sonderkommando force was regiment-sized, and he was rewarded for his criminality with the German Cross in gold. Even the man who bestowed that honour on him, the notorious Heinrich Himmler, described the unit as out of control, and complained that he had to keep replenishing it with new convicts because many of the unit fought among themselves and killed one another. He recounted an incident in which one member of the unit pulled a face at the idea of Germany winning the war, and was instantly shot by one of his fellow-soldiers. Corporal punishment was routinely used to keep the soldiers in line, often administered by Dirlewanger himself. He derived extreme pleasure from being in power, and from using that power to inflict suffering on others. This is sadism in its purest form, and it often goes hand in hand with a psychopathic mind.

Dirlewanger enjoyed something rare in the life-story of most psychopaths: almost unrestricted power. For as long as Germany occupied a subservient nation, he could act out his most inhuman desires. In August 1944, however, the German stranglehold over Belarus and eastern Russia was decisively broken. The Red Army's Operation Bagration inflicted staggering losses on Hitler's forces, and Dirlewanger's unit was one of those decimated. It was forced to retreat in the face of Soviet 'Deep Battle' tactics and after a desperate rearguard battle what remained of the force regrouped in Poland. Here reinforcements were hurriedly sent from other German-occupied lands. They were mostly hardened convicts plucked from concentration camps and prisons. A new 'storm force' was assembled, which now contained men just as violent and uncontrollable as the previous 'commandos'. Many were facing death sentences for hideous crimes and had nothing to lose by joining the maverick fighting unit. Above all, what remained unchanged was the man in charge: Oskar Dirlewanger, the drunken psychopath, now firmly addicted to alcohol, drugs and sadistic murder.

'The Butcher'

As the fortunes of war began to turn against the Nazis, more and more trouble spots emerged in their occupied lands, and Dirlewanger's unit was sent wherever vengeance was considered necessary. In August 1944 that meant Warsaw, the capital of Poland. An uprising there was threatening to overrun German positions and was tying down thousands of troops sorely needed elsewhere. Dirlewanger's job was to help crush the uprising and make an example of those responsible for it. He discharged his duties with barely concealed enthusiasm. Thousands of civilians were brutally slaughtered, and many more tortured. Women and children were raped and then killed.

Dirlewanger personally participated in the Wola Massacre, in which 40,000 civilians were shot, most over the course of just two days. He ordered three hospitals to be burnt to the ground with the patients still trapped inside. Nurses who fled the flames were stripped naked, whipped, raped and then hanged. Another 30,000 or more civilians were slaughtered as Dirlewanger rampaged through Warsaw's Old Town district. Many were burnt alive, others impaled on bayonets then hung out of windows.

Wherever there was bloodshed, there was Oskar Dirlewanger. Dressed in a long, black leather trench coat, he constantly urged his murdering henchmen forwards, inciting them to ever-greater acts of violence. Brandishing a revolver, he personally killed any of those who disobeyed, and sometimes even those he believed were not pushing forwards quickly enough. His own side referred to him as 'the Butcher'.

He took a hands-on approach to the summary executions held every Thursday, personally kicking the chairs from under those sentenced to hang. His men were fed vodka every morning and were almost always drunk by the time the bloodletting began. Dirlewanger found them less prone to question his orders that way. With the threat of death always hanging over them, the men learnt to do whatever their superior told them to. In one instance the order was to murder in cold blood some 350 children who were hiding in a school. Dirlewanger and his men walked through the building shooting them in the head, then smashing in their skulls with their rifle butts when they ran out of ammunition.

Dirlewanger not only tolerated the rape of women, he insisted upon it, and those who refused to engage in the practice were liable to be punished. One soldier who served alongside him later recalled that Dirlewanger threw a young Polish woman across a table in front of his men, and cut her open from stomach to throat with his bayonet as he raped her. Many historians have speculated that he was a necrophiliac who preferred to have sex with freshly deceased corpses. He also appeared to be particularly cruel towards children. One child that he snatched from a mother's arms was lifted high into the air and then thrown into a fire. Dirlewanger then shot the child's mother as she rushed forward to try and save her offspring. A one-legged boy was ordered to hop in front of the soldiers for their entertainment, until they grew bored of him and placed grenades into his bag. They roared with delight as he hopped away and was blown to smithereens.

Hatred of Christianity

Religion also appeared to be on Dirlewanger's long list of pet hates. He took particular pleasure in raping nuns, and went out of his way to torture priests and monks rather than execute them instantly as he often did with other civilians. One priest was tortured to death in his church as Dirlewanger's men got drunk on the sacred wine and urinated on the crucifixes. The church itself was ransacked and looted of its valuables. Unlike soldiers in standard German regiments, Dirlewanger's men were allowed to loot whenever and wherever they liked – as long as Dirlewanger himself had first pick of the most valuable items.

By October SS generals were begging their senior commanders to have Dirlewanger and his men transferred elsewhere. They were moved on to Slovakia to crush dissent there later the same year. The now familiar pattern of atrocities continued almost without a break. Indeed, Dirlewanger now received a further award from his superiors, this time the Knight's Cross of the Iron Cross. For the psychopath, respect and recognition are powerful motivators, and although those on the ground loathed Dirlewanger's tactics the support of the Nazi top brass encouraged him to continue with his barbarous methods. The only thing that could possibly end his insane power trip now was death. In February 1945 that was marching ever closer towards him, in the shape of the advancing Red Army. Dirlewanger's troops were sent to the front line to try to halt Stalin's advance. Used to fighting small bands of partisans or torturing unarmed civilians, the German convicts were no match for the battle-hardened and well-motivated Soviets. Dirlewanger was shot in the chest during the fighting, and evacuated out of the battle zone.

He survived the injury – his twelfth of the war. By the time he was able to leave hospital, however, it was clear that Germany was on the brink of losing the war. Dirlewanger went into hiding in Upper Swabia in the central south of Germany and donned civilian clothes. On 1 June 1945 he was arrested at a remote hunting lodge, where he was living under a false name. Unfortunately for Dirlewanger, he had a distinctive appearance: his painfully thin, gangly frame had led to him being nicknamed 'Gandhi' during the war. He was soon recognized by his captors as the notorious leader of the SS's most infamous death squad. Imprisoned in a camp at nearby Altshausen, he was guarded by Polish troops, all of whom knew exactly what crimes he had committed against their fellow-countrymen. Some time in early June he was discovered dead in his cell. Officially his death certificate states that he died of natural causes, but many who claim to have been eyewitnesses to his final days testified that he was beaten to death.

So horrific was the legacy left by Dirlewanger that for a time he haunted the world from beyond the grave. Until 1960, there were persistent reports that he had faked his death and joined the French Foreign Legion, with several people claiming to have seen him fighting during the First Indochina War or in Egypt or Syria. The Polish Government took the reports so seriously that Dirlewanger remained

on their official list of wanted criminals until an exhum-
ation of his grave took place in November 1960. It was
confirmed that the corpse in the ground was that of Oskar
Dirlewanger. He was subsequently reinterred, although
the exact place of his burial has never been made public
for fear of attracting macabre pilgrims.

Erzsébet Báthory – her beauty belied her true persona.

CHAPTER 5

ERZSÉBET BÁTHORY

On 29 December 1610, the King of Hungary's chief representative, György Thurzó, led a party of noblemen and men-at-arms in a raid of Castle Čachtice, the home of the wealthy Countess Erzsébet Báthory. György was the Palatine, or prime minister, of the country at the time, and had orders directly from the king to investigate reports of horrific murders taking place at the castle. The raiding party travelled in the utmost secrecy: they wanted to avoid a public scandal, and also sought to catch the countess red-handed if the reports proved to be true. What they discovered inside Castle Čachtice was a scene so gruesome that it gave rise to hundreds of folk tales about blood-drinking murderesses. It also resulted in one of the most sensational and macabre trials in history. The Hungarian court would hear testimony that Erzsébet Báthory tortured and murdered up to 650 young women behind the castle walls. This was no folk tale but the story of a real-life psychopath who killed entirely for pleasure, and entirely without remorse.

While many of the details of Báthory's life are lost in the mists of time, we do have a reasonably reliable account of the key events courtesy of Father Laslo Turáczi, who wrote a lengthy history of Hungary published in 1744. From this we learn that Báthory was born in August 1560, to one of the wealthiest and most influential families in Hungary – her cousin, in fact, was none other than György Thurzó, the representative sent by the king to investigate her. Several of her uncles had been *voivods* (princes) of Transylvania and another was a king in present-day Poland. She grew up on the family's lavish estate in Nyirbator, on the border between Hungary and Romania. Her family was of the Protestant faith – dangerous at a time when the majority of Hungarian noble families were Catholics.

Violent temper

From an early age Erzsébet suffered from blinding headaches and light-headedness, which we would today describe as migraines. She was also prone to seizures, and was probably epileptic. Above all, she was given to terrible fits of uncontrollable rage, and her violent temper was to remain a key characteristic throughout her life. It is possible her health issues were the result of generations of inbreeding within her family, though it may just have been genetic bad luck. At the time in question, nobles like Erzsébet wielded tremendous power over commoners, acting as judge and jury and answerable only to the king for their actions. Erzsébet would have grown up accustomed to seeing barbaric punishments being handed out by her family members to the peasants brought before them. One tale tells of a gypsy thief being sewn up inside the stomach of a horse with only his head protruding, then being left in that state to die.

Báthory's education was highly unusual: she had one. Most nobles could not read or write and used secretaries to handle all their necessary correspondence, but Erzsébet was well-read by the time she was in her teens, learning Latin and Greek as well as Hungarian, and studying mathematics, biology and astronomy. Women, in particular, were rarely educated to such a high standard, as their primary role was considered to be giving birth to male heirs. This was very much the idea when Erzsébet was engaged to be married at the age of 12 to Count Ferenc Nádasdy, at least four years her senior; some reports suggest he was much older. Nádasdy was dashing and brave, a fearsome warrior, but nowhere near as bright as his bride.

Like many psychopaths, Erzsébet was sexually active from an early age, and according to most reports she became pregnant during the summer of 1573. The father was not Count Nádasdy but another young nobleman called László (sometimes 'Ladisles') Bende. The story goes that when Nádasdy found out about the affair he had Bende castrated and then fed to his hounds: whether this is true or not, the daughter born to Báthory was never heard from again. The young couple's marriage went ahead on 8 May 1575 and thanks to the union of two powerful families they inherited more land than the king of Hungary. Nádasdy was known to be a harsh taskmaster who punished his servants for the slightest offence, and he may have taught Erzsébet the basics of physical violence, which she would later perfect herself.

Ferenc Nádasdy became a captain in the Hungarian army, and when the Ottoman Turks waged war against the country in 1578 he was called away to fight. He would be absent for extended periods throughout their marriage, leaving Báthory home alone, and answerable to no one but herself. Either as a result of her husband's frequent absences, or fertility problems (common among the inbred Hungarian nobility) Erzsébet failed to produce a legitimate heir for the first ten years of the marriage. She eventually gave birth to two sons, András and Pál, and three daughters, Anna, Orsolya and Katalin, but it is not known whether any of the children were the products of affairs. It is almost certain that her husband used the services of prostitutes while away on campaigns, as this was considered entirely reasonable for noble military men at the time. Erzsébet certainly had her pick of any male suitors who caught her eye: she was astonishingly beautiful, with long, dark hair and a perfect, milky-white complexion.

Mirror, mirror on the wall

With her great beauty came great vanity – another key characteristic of psychopaths. They tend to value superficial appearances over deeper virtues, due to their lack of empathy and emotional shallowness. Erzsébet went as far as designing her own full-length mirror that included armrests so that she could spend hours in front of it, leaning on the frame in comfort. She was rumoured to spend entire days gazing at herself as her hair was combed and made glossy by her servants. One enduring myth is that Erzsébet's bloodlust began after she slapped a servant and as a result got blood on her hands. It is said that she discovered that rubbing the blood on her skin made it appear soft and full of vitality. This tale grew to epic proportions, so that now many accounts of Báthory's life have her bathing in the blood of virgins; it is worth noting, however, that none of those who later spoke in court of her deeds ever mentioned any such bloodbaths. A more likely explanation is that the sight of blood simply excited her, and she drew sadistic pleasure from exercising the goddess-like power her nobility afforded her.

There were other key people in Erzsébet's life who profoundly influenced her. The first was her aunt, who was openly bisexual, and whom Erzsébet visited frequently for extended periods. The aunt encouraged her interest in witchcraft, and her uncle was also reportedly an alchemist and occultist. As so often in the story of Báthory it is difficult to separate fact from fiction, but a belief in supernatural evil forces was by no means uncommon at this time. Erzsébet also had several trusted employees who became key accomplices in her crimes. Her children's wet-nurse was called Dorothea Szentes, also known as Dorka, and was a peasant woman of great physical strength, believed by locals to be a witch. Her loyal manservant Johannes Ujvary, known as Ficzko, was later described as a dwarf and a cripple. An elderly washerwoman named Katalin Beneczky was also part of her cohort of servant-slayers. Erzsébet was undoubtedly the cruel mastermind behind the brutal murders and torture that occurred in the castle, but her slim build meant she needed the help of others to act out her deranged fantasies, which is where Dorka, Ficzko and Katalin came in.

A new scene and a new partner-in-crime

Under Erzsébet's instruction, maids and servants were routinely tortured and killed for the most minor of transgressions. While the peasant classes could expect rough treatment in almost any environment, the barbarity at Báthory's castle reached a level that caused outrage even to those inured to violence. Staff were lashed, beaten with barbed objects and cudgels, and dragged naked into the snow and doused with cold water, then left to freeze to death. It was not the consternation of the local population that caused Erzsébet to move her operations elsewhere, however, but the death of her husband. Some accounts suggest he died in battle in 1604, others that he contracted syphilis from a prostitute or was murdered by one for not paying her. Whichever is true, his widow moved almost immediately to a second castle at Čachtice, in modern-day Slovakia. The building was a wedding present from the Nádasdy family, and became the scene of Erzsébet Báthory's most infamous crimes.

Here she joined forces with a new partner in crime. Little is known of Anna Darvulia or exactly how she came to meet Erzsébet Báthory. Most accounts describe her as a witch, many suggest she was Báthory's lesbian lover; all agree that she was the most violent sadist in Erzsébet's entourage. Psychopaths tend to be drawn to those who reflect their own perversions back to them, and this is

An artist's impression of Erzsébet Báthory watching as young women are tortured in front of her.

certainly what happened in the relationship between the two women in Castle Čachtice. For the next five years they indulged in a litany of violence against young girls, for the sole reason that it gave them pleasure.

Most of the victims were between 10 and 15 years old. A carriage drawn by black horses would leave the castle gates to scour the village for the most attractive young girls, who could be lured back with the promise of paid employment. Few questioned why the castle required such a large number of staff, or why so few were ever heard of again. This was a period where speaking ill of the nobility could cost you your life.

Even so, as the years went by and the black carriage took more and more young girls away, word began to spread. Not all the deaths could be explained away with the official line that they were due to cholera. Peasants too frightened to speak to anyone else confided in their priests. The priests in turn had contacts with the lower nobility, and thus the story of the 'Castle of Blood' slowly began to spread. In the dungeons, it was said, the girls were tied up, then beaten until their limbs swelled horribly. Then Erzsébet Báthory would have their clothes changed so that she could watch them stain with blood all over again when the beatings restarted. Some had their limbs cut off, others were cut and tortured with razor-sharp blades, several were burnt alive. It is reported that monks in a neighbouring monastery used to throw pans against the walls in order to drown out the sound of the tortured girls' screams.

Foul tortures

There was no apparent end to the novel tortures that Báthory delighted in devising for her wretched victims. The mindset of the psychopath is unlimited by any morality. She sewed their mouths shut, or forced them to eat strips of their own skin. In the early hours of a torture session, she pierced them with needles to inflict as much pain as possible without causing serious injury or death. She would burn their genitals and nipples with the flame from a candle. Then she would bite the flesh of her victims, tearing away huge chunks with her teeth. Almost always, these acts of torture were merely the prelude to what most excited her: cold-blooded murder.

Anna Darvulia died in 1609. True psychopaths rarely dwell in grief for long, however, and Erzsébet soon replaced Anna with a local widow, Erzsi Majorova. Again, exactly how the two came to meet is lost to us, but it is clear from subsequent events that Erzsi was hand-picked to be compliant, and perhaps encouraging of the barbarous crimes that Erzsébet was by now addicted to committing. Indeed, Erzsi seems to have been responsible for expanding the pool of victims from local peasant girls to members of the local nobility. Perhaps there were simply too few peasant girls left, or perhaps Erzsébet had grown bored of torturing those she considered to be her inferiors. A constant need for new stimulation and novelty is another common trait in psychopaths. Risk-taking is yet another – and by snatching noble women Báthory was certainly taking a major new risk. Peasants were considered to be chattel, the possessions of their employers, to be treated however the employer wished; but nobles were viewed very differently. However, the reason psychopaths are such risk-takers is linked to their grandiose sense of themselves: they believe they are infallible and immortal. In short, they simply cannot imagine that they will ever get caught.

Báthory opened an 'academy of etiquette' in 1609, ostensibly to educate and refine the manners of young noblewomen. Before long, the young women began to disappear, and their parents were refused access to them. While the bodies of peasants could be disposed of without too much trouble, noble families did not treat death so lightly, and insisted on investigating the loss of their loved ones. Complaints poured in to the King's Court, and György Thurzó was forced to respond. By 1610 the reports of strange and terrifying events at the castles owned by Erzsébet Báthory were becoming too numerous to ignore. A member of the Lutheran clergy, Istvan Magyari, publicly raised the matter of the girls' disappearances in his sermons. When Ferenc was alive, Báthory had some protection from prosecution because the nobleman had lent the Hungarian crown a vast amount of money. Now that he was dead, however, that fact worked against his widow: it was in the king's interest to see that huge loan liquidated.

Crimes uncovered

It was not the done thing to investigate such serious matters publicly, so Thurzó began by negotiating with two of Báthory's son-in-laws to ensure that Erzsébet's daughters were not dragged in to the scandal swirling around their mother. They agreed that they would place their errant mother-in-law in a convent, rather than have her face trial for her crimes. With that agreement secured, Thurzó organized the raiding party that arrived at Castle Čachtice on 29 December 1610. They found Báthory in the process of torturing a girl, with another lying badly wounded nearby. In the same dungeon they found the bodies of two more girls. Báthory was seized and confined within the castle while the full extent of her barbarism was explored. Thurzó's search party apparently found bodies wherever they looked in the castle, many without eyes or limbs. Dogs ran through the halls with human body parts in their mouths. One body was found partially burnt in a fireplace. Dozens more were buried in shallow graves in the castle grounds.

Surviving victims were rounded up and interviewed under oath. Báthory's accomplices were also interrogated, and realizing their lives were now on the line they attempted to outdo one another in the fulsomeness of their testimony, hoping clemency might result. A special tribunal was held on 2 January 1611, in front of 21 judges, with Theodosius de Szulo of the Royal Supreme Court presiding. Báthory herself was not in attendance: she was, despite all that had happened, still considered a noble, and too illustrious to appear in a common court. Each of Báthory's cohorts was called to testify in turn, however, being asked the same 11 questions relating to who they had harmed, what they had done and who assisted them in the crimes.

Ficzko the dwarf confessed to helping kill 37 girls, though he couldn't remember the total including adults, presumably because he had lost count. He claimed that Dorka cut the fingers off many victims one by one. Ilona Joo, Báthory's childhood nurse, told of torturing girls with red-hot pokers and believed she had killed around 50 this way. Similarly appalling testimony was heard from the others accused – Dorka, Erzsi Majorova and Katalin Beneczky. All of them implicated Erzsébet in the murders, and accused her of being the mastermind behind the 'Castle of Blood'. A register, written in Báthory's own hand, listed the names of 650 girls who were all believed to have perished. In the end, on the basis of the human remains found in and around the castle, she and the others were found guilty on 80 counts of murder.

Solitary confinement

In the light of such damning testimony, clemency was never likely to be on the agenda for those not of noble birth: Ficzko was beheaded and the rest were burnt at the stake. Báthory herself was spared a death sentence, being instead confined to the tower at her own castle for the rest of her life. Like most psychopaths, she expressed absolutely no remorse for her crimes. Instead, she continued to protest her total innocence, claiming that all 650 of the women who had died in her castles did so of natural causes. It is common for psychopaths to behave as if any punishment handed down to them is in fact a terrible injustice, and this is exactly how Báthory reacted to her sentence. She petitioned everyone she could for a reprieve. But the king himself had to be dissuaded from executing her, and she had already received all the mercy she was going to get. The windows and doors of her room were bricked shut, leaving just a narrow slit through which she was handed food and water. After three and a half years of confinement, she died.

Conditions were harsh for Báthory during those final years, and we do not know the exact circumstances of her death. It is fair to say, however, that the stress of solitary confinement would have been felt more acutely by someone with a psychopathic personality than by someone who was psychologically normal. Psychopaths crave stimulation and novelty, and live for the next new exciting sensation. Deprived of all this, it appears Báthory rapidly sank into despair. Long after her lonely death, however, she achieved a kind of immortality that would doubtless have thrilled her, inspiring countless folk tales of blood-drinking vampires who dwelt in dark castles. The reality was stranger than any fiction, and even 500 years later Erzsébet Báthory remains history's most egregious example of a deranged and sadistic female psychopath.

Robert Philip Hanssen.

CHAPTER 6

ROBERT PHILIP HANSSEN

Robert Philip Hanssen is considered by many to be the worst traitor in modern American history. In return for money and diamonds, the former FBI agent passed highly classified US government documents, including nuclear war plans, to the former Soviet Union and Russia. One of the ways the US responded to this devastating breach of security was to fund a study that sought to understand the psychology of Hanssen. The idea was that if the government could find a way to 'get inside his mind' they might be able to spot future spies and informants before they have the chance to wreak the kind of havoc Hanssen caused. The report by J. Scott Sanford described Hanssen's actions as acts of 'seemingly inexplicable psychopathic violence'. How did one of the FBI's star agents come to betray his own country and jeopardize the safety of the entire population of the United States? To answer that we must look for the clues that so often emerge with the benefit of hindsight. In the case of Hanssen, as with many psychopaths, the story starts with a troubled childhood.

Perhaps tellingly, the young Hanssen's favourite comic strip as a child was the 'Spy versus Spy' cartoons in *Mad* magazine. Duplicity and trickery appealed to him from an early age. He read voraciously – not just cartoons but also adult books of every description. An only child whose father was often away on service in the Navy, he escaped into the pages of detective novels, spy thrillers and horror stories. He developed an interest in ham radio, preferring to interact with distant voices than real-life classmates, who described him as having an air of self-importance as if he were above their childish games.

Hanssen was born on 18 April 1944 in Chicago, Illinois, to a family of mixed Danish-Polish and German descent. After the war ended his father returned to the family home and joined the Chicago police. Perhaps his experiences in the Second World War had hardened him, or perhaps he just missed a crucial bonding period with his son, but either way Howard Hanssen was an emotionally distant father to young Robert. He was very much a 'man's man' and his macho attitude did not seem to gel with the sensitive boy who loved books.

Mean and macho father

Howard Hanssen was detailed to Chicago police's infamous 'Red Squad', which monitored the local population for signs of communism, subversion and anarchism. Robert grew up during the McCarthy period of near-hysterical anti-communism and scares of 'reds under the bed'. It is impossible not to read his later actions in providing secrets to his father's most hated and feared enemies as something personal between a father and a son. In paying back his father for the perceived injustices inflicted upon him, Robert Hanssen also placed the lives of 319 million Americans in jeopardy. This demonstrates an alarming lack of perspective, proportionality or justice. That is something often seen in the psychopathic mindset: the inability to empathize with victims leads to a reckless disregard for any 'collateral damage' caused by the individual's actions.

The kind of relationship Robert had with his father can be illustrated by a couple of documented incidents from his childhood. When Robert was six or seven years old, his father spun him around until he became dizzy and vomited. Then he rubbed Robert's face in the vomit so that he could smell and taste 'what defeat was like'. Several years later, Howard Hanssen deliberately arranged for his son to fail his driving test. Perhaps this was a misguided attempt to 'toughen up' his bookish son. All it succeeded in doing was instilling a deep-seated resentment in him instead. Throughout his childhood, Robert was the butt of Howard's jokes and disparaging abuse. He may well have felt a sense of liberation when he finally left the family home to study chemistry at Knox College in Galesburg, Illinois, in 1966.

At college he continued his interest in the writings of Karl Marx, and elected to study Russian as one of his course modules. He became obsessed with the autobiography of the notorious British spy and traitor Kim Philby, *My Silent War*, recommending the book to friends. He also applied to become a cryptographer at the National Security Agency (NSA), but his application was declined. Many psychopaths jump from one area of interest to another erratically, particularly when young, and this pattern is evident in Hanssen's college years. He wanted to become a doctor, then studied dentistry, then finally switched to business studies after three years. Another trait common to psychopaths also came to the fore in Hanssen's college years: he developed a reputation as a daring risk-taker. He would often race his car with others, screeching around tight corners and ignoring stop signs, traffic lights and speed limits. On one occasion at a friend's house he fired a rifle into a bullet-trap at such short range that shards of concrete flew across the room.

Policeman – in his father's footsteps

Hanssen had a brilliant mind when he cared to use it, but his anti-authoritarian streak often meant his studies suffered. He walked out of one exam because he didn't care for the question, but it didn't matter to his grades since he had worked out a cunning way of getting the high marks he felt were rightfully his. He broke into an administrative building and altered his school records. Duplicity and cheating, he had learnt, were far easier routes to success than hard work and honest endeavour. Hanssen graduated with an MBA in accounting and information systems, but he yearned for more excitement from life and, tellingly, he followed his father's footsteps into the Chicago Police Department. It was a decision that infuriated Howard Hanssen, who had always dreamed that his son would become a doctor, and had repeatedly warned him that he was not cut out for a career in law enforcement.

Robert specialized in Forensic Accounting at Chicago P.D., and was tasked with investigating corruption and unethical practices. As his father had predicted, he didn't fit in. His superiors didn't trust him from the outset, suspecting he was an undercover agent sent to gather information on the force. Hanssen was more highly qualified than most recruits, and was described by fellow-officers as glib and slick – adjectives that come up time and again in the description of classic psychopaths. When, four years later, his application to join the FBI was accepted and he moved to Gary, Indiana, to take up his new post, few at Chicago P.D. were sorry to see him go. In Robert Hanssen's mind, however, he had succeeded in his ambition to out-do his father, and he was now moving on to bigger and better things.

In tow was the woman he had married in 1968, Bernadette 'Bonnie' Wauck. She would later become entangled in the deceit and lies that characterized Hanssen's personality, but their early years together were relatively happy. That was largely because Hanssen was already an expert in deception. Within days of their wedding Bonnie had discovered he was having an affair with an ex-girlfriend, but he begged for forgiveness and swore he would be faithful thereafter. In fact, he continued to have affairs and sleep with prostitutes; he just made sure that his wife would never again find out about it.

Opus Dei and GRU

One lasting impression Bonnie made on Robert concerned her religious faith: Bonnie was a Roman Catholic and Robert converted to her faith soon after meeting her, despite having been raised a Lutheran. He became a devout follower of the Catholic faith and began to attend meetings of the controversial Opus Dei institution. Critics of Opus Dei describe it as a secretive and elitist organization, and it featured heavily (in fictionalized form) in the novel and film *The Da Vinci Code*. It is easy to see how a clandestine and enigmatic club-like structure would appeal to the personality of Robert Hanssen. His Catholic faith provided the additional release of regular confession and absolution, too.

In 1978 Hanssen and his family, which now included three of the six children he would eventually have, moved to New York. He was detailed to work in counter-intelligence, with specific responsibility for the compilation of a database of suspected Soviet intelligence agents. Within a year of taking up the new post, Hanssen was reaching out to the Glavnoye razvedyvatel'noye upravleniye or GRU, the main intelligence directorate of the Soviet Union. The Soviets, naturally, were delighted to make his acquaintance.

The mystery of why Hanssen made such an audacious and treacherous approach at this time will probably never be answered. He later claimed that his sole motivation was money. If this were true, however, he would have asked for far more cash and diamonds (he was certainly worth more to the Soviets). Instead he was content to have money placed in an offshore bank account that deep down he knew he would never be able to access without revealing his identity. It seems as though this illusion of wealth was more important to Hanssen than actual wealth, money that he could spend and enjoy. To Hanssen money was a way of 'keeping score'; a measure of his value to his GRU handlers. And, starved of admiration or encouragement from an early age, Hanssen needed above all else to know that he was valued. In the FBI he was just another agent – in the GRU he was a star. The name of 'Ramon Garcia' would, in time, become legendary: it was the codename Hanssen chose for himself when he elected to become a Soviet spy.

His worst betrayals were still ahead of him, but even at this early stage Hanssen must have known that the information he was passing on could have fatal consequences for those named by him. One of the earliest casualties of his spying was a general in the Soviet Army, codenamed by the Americans 'Tophat'. Hanssen informed the Soviets that the man's real name was Dmitri Polyakov. They didn't act on the information immediately so as to preserve Hanssen's cover, but when the same man was betrayed by a second American mole called Aldrich Ames in 1985, Polyakov was arrested. Two years later he stood trial and was executed. The Soviets had eliminated an American spy, and managed to keep their own spies safe. The existence of two Soviet spies – Ames at the CIA and Hanssen at the FBI – complicated the American counterintelligence operation. After the arrest of Ames in 1994, investigators believed they had rid themselves of their 'leak', which made them complacent about investigating any further. As a result, Hanssen flourished.

Success at the FBI

One of the psychopath's distinct 'career phases', well-documented in psychology literature, is what is called 'the manipulation phase'. During this period the psychopath plays the role of an ideal employee, constantly seeking recognition from power-holders, and support and adulation from peers. The psychopath is really acting as a 'puppet-master' during this phase, enjoying the manipulation he can perform, while awaiting the opportunity to twist the trust placed in him as a result of his 'good behaviour'. Robert Hanssen's work at the FBI is a textbook example of this. He appeared to be diligent and trustworthy, and his sensitive work resulted in him being granted senior-level security clearance, including un-restricted access to vast stores of highly classified information.

Despite his best efforts and undoubted aptitude, Hanssen failed to receive the respect he felt he deserved from his colleagues. Fellow agents thought him odd, and he made few close friends in the agency. He was referred to as 'Dr Death' and 'the Mortician' due to his penchant for only ever wearing stiffly starched black suits. He did not socialize with his workmates, and was not considered helpful or cooperative when they made requests of him. Even after several years of working alongside him, many later reflected that they did not feel as though they knew what made him tick. Colleagues described him as 'superficial' and an FBI division chief summed him up as 'a lurker', hovering at the side of any gathering. Had they viewed Hanssen with the eyes of a psychologist, they would have seen the tell-tale signs of a psychopathic mind. Psychopaths' inability to empathize is what leads them to appear superficial and distant to others. They can be amiable, and even charming, but only because they have learnt to mimic such behaviour by keenly observing others. In the end, they do not come across as natural or open and any charm they possess is only ever skin-deep.

First suspicions

To a psychopath, adoration from others is a prime requisite. Their ego is simply too large to allow them to function as a 'team player', and they rapidly feel undervalued if they are not considered a 'star'. Hanssen craved ever greater power, and when he did not get it from within he crossed over to the Soviet side, where they would pander to his need for adulation. He was careful never to reveal his true identity to his Soviet handlers, communicating through a series of anonymous

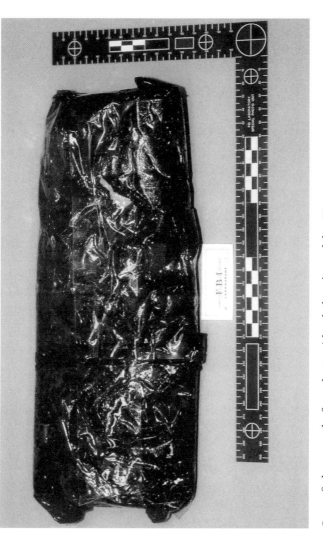

One of the parcels found at a 'dead drop' used by Hanssen.

letters. Information was exchanged by using a simple system of 'dead drops', where Hanssen would leave classified information at a pre-arranged place and time. In return he received cash payments and packets of diamonds, and the most important reward of all, the constant indulgent praise of his intelligence and skill.

All went well until 1980, when his wife Bonnie caught him counting out $20,000 in used $100 bills and confronted Robert about where it had come from. He did what most psychopaths would do in such a situation: he lied through his teeth. He told her he had been selling the Soviets worthless information and promised he would pay the money to charity and refrain from leaking any more secrets. He duly confessed to his Opus Dei priest, Robert Bucciarelli, and made some contributions to charity, though he skimmed off a hefty percentage of the amount he had promised to pay. Hanssen's brother-in-law learnt of the fact he kept large amounts of cash at home and reluctantly reported it to his bosses – he, too, was an FBI agent. However, no formal investigation into Hanssen was launched: he was such a diligent worker that he remained above suspicion.

Major leaks to Soviets

A year later Hanssen was moved to Washington and his security clearance was raised to 'Above Top Secret'. He kept his head down and broke off relations with his Soviet handlers for a while, until after four years of apparently solid work he was moved back to New York. In October 1985 the lure of espionage work became too great and he once again reached out to the communist regime. This time he sent a letter to Victor Cherkashin, the head of the Soviet espionage operation in Washington, via a KGB colonel he knew he could trust. He asked for $100,000 in return for information about three double agents working for US intelligence. Hanssen got the money and the three US spies – Sergey Motorin, Valeriy Martynov and Boris Yuzhin – were arrested. Motorin and Martynov were sentenced to death, and Yuzhin was given a six-year prison sentence. This was the true price of Robert Hanssen's ego trip. Two years after betraying the men he was, ironically, placed in charge of the investigation to find out who had leaked their identities.

Hanssen continued to provide valuable information to the Soviets over the course of the next few years. He told them of a secret FBI tunnel under the Soviet embassy that could be used to listen to conversations in the building. He outlined all the Measurement and Signature Intelligence (MASINT) capabilities of the United States. He tipped off the KGB that one of their agents, Felix Bloch, was about to be arrested. The only break in the flow of secrets came when the Soviet Union collapsed in December 1991. Even then, however, Hanssen was not out of commission for long: he began leaking information to the newly formed Russian Federation the following year.

In 1993 Hanssen hacked into the computer of a fellow FBI agent, just to prove that it was insecure. A keen computer geek, he was almost undone by his love of probing around in 1997, when IT personnel discovered a password-cracking program on his computer. Hanssen coolly lied his way out of the situation by claiming he was trying to use a colour printer in the office that was password-protected. The near miss did nothing to make him desist from his activities, and he continued regularly to hack into FBI computers to check whether he was under investigation. He wasn't. The FBI and CIA joint mole-hunting team believed the leaks were coming from Brian Kelley, a CIA operative. They interrogated him and then publicly accused him of being 'Graysuit', their code name for the mole. He remained on administrative leave for two years until Hanssen was finally arrested.

Caught on tape

That arrest was made possible not by an internal investigation but by buying the information from a former KGB agent, who gave the investigators Hanssen's name. By this time the FBI and CIA were so desperate they were willing to pay the informant a staggering $7 million for the information. At first they literally could not believe it. The informant included an audiotape of 'Graysuit' arranging a dead-drop, however, and the voice was confirmed to be that of Robert Hanssen. They placed him under round-the-clock surveillance and provided him with a brand new assistant – one who was an undercover agent of their own. Eric O'Neill was the rookie FBI agent tasked with obtaining the 'smoking gun' of Hanssen's Palm III Personal Digital Assistant computer. He managed to do so while Hanssen was called away for gun training, and once the FBI downloaded and decrypted the information on it they had everything they needed for a prosecution.

Hanssen was arrested while making a dead-drop in Virginia's Foxstone Park. Upon being placed in handcuffs he remarked, 'What took you so long?' It was one last sneering attempt to assert his superiority over his peers, and it illustrates again his need to feel superior, even while being caught committing a crime. When shown the evidence against him, Hanssen immediately agreed to a plea bargain, and assisted the authorities in return for a guarantee that he would not face the death penalty. He was sentenced to 15 consecutive life sentences on 10 May 2002. In court he apologized for his behaviour and claimed to be ashamed of himself. That may be, in part, due to the scandalous revelations concerning his sexual proclivities that emerged during the investigation. It transpired that

THE 10 WORST PSYCHOPATHS

not only had Hanssen betrayed the FBI and the country, but he had also betrayed the trust of his wife in the most heinous way imaginable.

Sexual betrayals

Many psychopaths are also voyeurs, as they are, by their very nature, outsiders. Hanssen took this trait to a grotesque new level, however, by installing hidden cameras in his bedroom and allowing his friend to watch him have sex with his wife, Bonnie. Hanssen saw Jack Hoschouer as a 'real man' because he had served in Vietnam and had many more sexual partners than Robert. He invited Jack to watch him have sex live, from the family television in the den. He also posted pictures of Bonnie naked on the Internet. There was one credible report that he planned to give her a date-rape drug so that Hoschauer could sexually assault or rape her. He and Hoschauer hired prostitutes and participated in group-sex orgies together. Hanssen's own sister-in-law refused ever to be alone with him after he touched her exposed breast while she fed her child. He was preoccupied with hardcore pornography, and visited strip-clubs regularly. For a period of two years he had an affair with a female dancer he met at one such club, Priscilla Galey. All of these matters would have been of grave concern to his superiors had they known about them, because they opened him up to the possibility of blackmail. As it transpired, it was the lure of excitement rather than the threat of exposure that caused him to betray his country.

In total it is thought that Hanssen was responsible for betraying at least 25 agents, many of whom paid for his treachery with their liberty or their lives. In return he received approximately $1.6 million in cash and diamonds. National security authorities describe Hanssen's breach of classified information as the most devastating in the United States' history. Although he apologized to his wife and family, he expressed no remorse whatsoever towards the FBI, the individuals who died because of his actions, or the nation whose security he so recklessly endangered. He summed himself up with the following words: 'I am like Dr Jekyll and Mr Hyde, and sometimes Mr Hyde takes over.'

In one of his letters to his handlers he pondered on his own psychological make-up, which demonstrates he was fully aware of the gravity of his crimes and the risks he was taking. 'One might propose that I am either insanely brave or quite insane,' he wrote to the Soviets. 'I'd answer neither. I'd say, insanely loyal. Take your pick. There is insanity in all the answers.'

Jim Jones (seated, centre) and his wife, Marceline (seated, left), his adopted family and his sister-in-law (seated, right) and her three children.

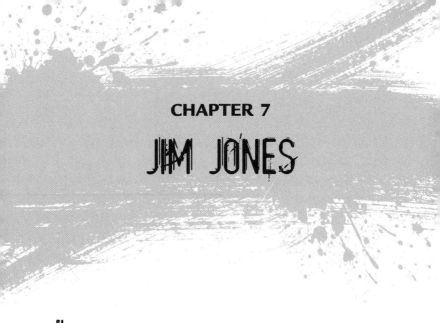

CHAPTER 7

JIM JONES

In November 1978, at the South American settlement known as Jonestown, 909 people died as the result of a mass murder–suicide. Most of them had travelled from the West Coast of the United States and, excluding natural disasters, the subsequent events constituted the greatest loss of civilian life in American history. Even today, only the tragic events of 11 September 2001 led to greater slaughter. Many of the victims were children, murdered by their middle-class professional parents. How could such a monstrous massacre happen? The answer lies in the extraordinary psychopathic personality of the cult's leader, Jim Jones.

James Warren 'Jim' Jones was born in Randolph County, Indiana, in 1931, and grew up in nearby Lynn in a humble shack without plumbing or electricity. He was the son of James Thurman Jones, a disabled First World War veteran, and his wife Lynetta, who apparently believed that she had given birth to the messiah. James Thurman was a racist alcoholic who attended Ku Klux Klan meetings in the poor and deeply racially divided town. Even during the Great Depression, when many households struggled to make ends meet, the Jones family were the poorest of the poor.

It was a source of intense shame to Jim that his father did not work and that the government assistance the family relied on was so meagre. His mother encouraged him to educate himself so as not to suffer the same fate as James Thurman.

Young preacher

A bookish boy, Jones read voraciously and had a precocious interest in the lives and works of Hitler, Stalin and Karl Marx. Above all, however, the young Jim Jones read the Bible, and as a result became a pious and deeply religious child. This made Jones a somewhat dull child to be around in a world where children had to make their own entertainment. He had an extreme aversion to dirt, which excluded him from the rough and tumble of most playground games. He hectored 'sinners' outside the local pool hall and preached on street corners, dressed in a white sheet; he was regularly bullied and teased as a result. The already socially awkward child became more and more insular and lonely. When he did bring a friend home to visit, it was a fellow-outsider, the son of the sole African-American family in Lynn at that time. James Thurman refused to allow the boy into the house, causing a poisonous rift with Jim that lasted for many years. By the time he left home for college, Jim had become as different from his father as he could possibly be: given James Thurman's extreme right-wing views, this meant Jim becoming a devoted communist.

The young man had also learnt the importance of control. He had none in the family home, and was an outsider at school, but he managed to build his own small community of religious zealots in the loft at the back of his house. There he would preach for hours, refusing to let his restless congregation of peers leave, and even firing a .45 calibre handgun at one who did so. Deprived of love or understanding, the young Jim Jones had developed a seething anger that now morphed into a need to dominate and control others. He also demonstrated a cruel and sadistic streak: as a child he frequently held elaborate funerals for small animals, and when none were available to bury he reportedly killed some himself. His propensity for violence and his domineering personality were brilliantly masked, however, by a superficial warm charm and apparent interest in social justice.

The People's Temple

After his parents separated, Jim Jones moved with his mother to Richmond, Indiana. He became a student pastor at Somerset Methodist Church, but quickly fell out with the church leadership over the issue of racial segregation. Jones passionately believed in integration, and in the 1950s in the United States this was a minority view. He resolved to found his own church, and funded his dream by selling imported monkeys as pets door to door. His religious services soon attracted local African-American and white liberal residents in large numbers and in 1956 the People's Temple was officially opened in Indianapolis. By then Jones had met and married nurse Marceline Baldwin, the daughter of a prominent Richmond couple who were well-liked and respected for their charity work. They had one child together and adopted six others, of various nationalities, referring to themselves as a 'rainbow family'.

From the outset, Jones's sermons stressed the importance of loyalty – though he dressed that up as 'unity'. He preached that the congregation owed primary allegiance not to their families or friends but to God – and God's representative on earth, namely Jim Jones. With the grandiose sense of self-importance so typical of the psychopath, Jones began to claim he had the power to heal the sick. Indeed, he went so far as to say that no member of his congregation had ever died. When local authorities began investigating these healing rituals, Jones decided to move his entire church out of state. He chose Redwood Valley, just north of Ukiah in northern California, after reading an article in *Esquire* magazine that listed it as one of the safest places to live in the event of a nuclear attack. His paranoid delusion that the end of the world was at hand is evident even at this relatively early stage of his career. He claimed to see visions of nuclear holocausts in Indianapolis and Chicago. After visiting Brazil and Guyana as possible other places of safety, he told his congregation he was certain that the world would end on 15 July 1967. In the aftermath, he said, he would become the leader of a new socialist utopia.

'Trust bandit'

Around 65 families followed Jones to California, but in the more liberal environment of the United States' West Coast in the 1960s the numbers soon swelled. Jones wisely branched out into the San Francisco Bay Area, at that time a haven for the peace-loving alternative lifestyles of the hippies, and he set up homes for the elderly and mentally ill. Psychopaths are sometimes described as 'trust bandits' due to their habit of ensnaring victims by first gaining their trust, and Jones's high-profile charity work is a classic example of this tactic in action. He was lauded by the press and those in political power for his social work, but in reality this was just the first part of a much larger scheme. That scheme would ultimately lead to tragedy in Jonestown. Unbeknown to the outside world, the People's Temple was evolving into a cult, with Jim Jones as its psychopathic messiah.

The tenor of Jones's speeches became more political, more overtly communist, and members were now expected to show their loyalty by devoting all of their material wealth to Jones. He demanded that his congregation refer to him as 'Father', and he ruthlessly punished any who showed signs of dissent. Jones used his religious power for political leverage, bussing in his congregation and ordering them to vote for his favoured candidate in the San Francisco mayoral elections. In return he was given access to high-powered politicians with a great deal of influence. For a psychopath, power and attention are addictive, and Jones was by now getting plenty of both. He began to enjoy a party lifestyle of drink and drugs – totally at odds to the values he was espousing in his sermons. But the egocentric cult leader clearly did not believe that any rules should apply to him. He took sexual advantage of the vulnerable women in the congregation, telling them his love would purify them as he raped them.

Partly as a result of his drug-taking and partly because he was simply high on power, Jones's behaviour became increasingly erratic. He had paranoid delusions of conspiracies being hatched against him, and suffered violent mood swings, from ecstatic highs to angry, violent lows. Several times there were reports of shots being fired in the grand new home of the People's Temple, 'Happy Acres' Ranch. Nobody seemed keen to investigate the powerful cult, however, and any difficult questions were answered by Jones's slick team of PR experts who dismissed any criticisms as 'hate-mongering'. Jones came to believe he was the reincarnation of Mahatma Gandhi or (depending on his mood) Jesus Christ, Buddha or Vladimir Lenin. The psychopath almost always believes that he is destined for greatness, chosen by destiny to change the world.

Back in Indianapolis, local reporter Carolyn Pickering received a letter from a concerned relative whose daughter was a cult member in California. She began to investigate, teaming up with the *San Francisco Examiner*'s Rev. Lester Kinsolving, who wrote a column for the paper called 'Inside Religion'. On 10 September 1972, the pair visited Jones in Redwood and observed the cult members first hand. Jim Jones did his best to flatter and charm them, warmly praising their work as he guided them on a tour of his temple. He was by now 41 years old, wearing his trademark dark glasses to hide the bags under his eyes, and dressed in a fashionable white turtleneck jumper. But the reporters saw through his smarmy façade and reported the truth: armed guards patrolled the perimeter of the compound, under-age children were married off against their will, and Jones himself was an egomaniac who claimed to be able to raise the dead.

Power-crazed

Jones reacted in the only way the psychopath can: he went on the offensive. He sent 150 members of the People's Temple to march up and down outside the offices of the *Examiner* holding placards denouncing the paper. His lawyers threatened to sue. The paper declined to print any further stories about the cult, and the police took no action over the numerous suspicious 'suicides' of cult members. Jim Jones had faced down his critics, and won. People with a normal psychological make-up would view such an incident as a warning that they are sailing too close to the wind, but psychopaths merely become emboldened by their perceived triumphs. Jones was gradually coming to feel invincible, as well as immortal.

That feeling of invincibility was doubtless magnified in December 1973 when Jim Jones was arrested in a cinema in Los Angeles for homosexual activity, but the charges were dropped and the record sealed. Jones had friends in high places, and could afford to indulge in such risky public behaviour. Allegations of strange goings on at the People's Temple did still surface from time to time, and there were several defections, but for the most part Jones managed to keep the worst of his excesses away from public scrutiny. He was exerting ever more control over his followers, forcing them to drink wine that he claimed was laced with poison in order to test their loyalty to him. To be a true believer meant being prepared to die for Jim Jones. Again we see the psychopathic mindset at work: power is everything to a psychopath, and the ultimate power is that over life and death.

The creation of Jonestown

In June 1974, the first 'pioneers' took a flight out to Georgetown in Guyana, and journeyed from there to the settlement soon to become infamous across the world as Jonestown. They would spend the next three years clearing land and constructing the new temple complex in the South American jungle.

Back in California, Jones continued to expand his church and extend his control over his followers. He moved the church's headquarters into the centre of San Francisco. Increasingly obsessed with the coming end of the world, he took his followers on brutal trips out into the wilderness for what he called 'survival training'. His aim was to turn his peaceful congregation into a well-oiled military machine that could take over the country once the holocaust was over. Even children were not spared: on one occasion the four-year-old Tommy Kice was forced to eat even though he insisted he was not hungry. When he later vomited, Jones forced him to eat his own vomit as punishment. It is an eerie echo of the punishment that the psychopath Robert Hanssen received at the hands of his tyrannical father. The aim was utter humiliation, control through terror.

In 1977, *San Francisco Chronicle* journalist Marshall Kilduff wrote an exposé of the cult which the paper refused to publish. He took the story to *New West* magazine, which published his allegations of physical, sexual and emotional abuse in full. For Jim Jones the article was further proof of his paranoid conspiracy theory – that the establishment was out to destroy him. Believing the United States was destined to be wiped off the face of the earth very shortly, he decided the time was right to move his congregation to the safety of the jungle in Guyana. His dream of 'pure communism' would be turned into reality in the summer of 1977. Naturally, Jim Jones would be the tyrannical leader of this 'community of equals', managing what he called their 'translation' from this world to another planet which he claimed they would travel to after all dying together.

Jonestown investigated

The sudden departure of the cult members beyond the jurisdiction of the United States alarmed the relatives of those involved, however. Several ex-cult members formed a Concerned Relatives group and lobbied Congress to take action. In June 1978, Temple member Deborah Layton escaped from Jonestown and brought with her eyewitness reports of the living conditions there. Her testimony made for lurid headlines in the press, and the tide of public opinion began to turn against Jim Jones. California congressman Leo Ryan decided to get to the bottom of the allegations by visiting Jonestown and seeing for himself whether it was a jungle paradise or a hellhole created by a psychopathic cult leader. His plane touched down at the Guyanese capital of Georgetown on 15 November 1978, and from there he flew on to the remote airstrip at Port Kaituma. The final part of the journey to Jonestown was completed in the back of a dump truck.

The congressman and his team were nervous: they were a long way from home and the Reverend Jim Jones was accused of being a tyrannical lunatic who ruled his community with a ruthless determination. Leo Ryan and his legislative aide, Jackie Speier, had both made their last will and testament before departure. Armed guards patrolled the high perimeter fences of Jones's compound. At first the visit appeared to be going well – Jones organized an elaborate welcoming ceremony and Congressman Ryan was given a guided tour of the settlement, replete with gushing praise from Jim Jones's hand-picked loyal followers. He announced to a cheering congregation that he was impressed by what he saw. But the reception party turned sour when Ryan was handed a note written by a cult member who was desperate to escape the jungle prison. Ryan showed the note to Jones, whose mood suddenly changed. The paranoid psychopath saw his carefully created façade of utopian communism crumble before the world's media. The insult was too treasonous to bear.

Control through terror

Initially, he continued his staged act as the benevolent leader, as the psychopath is wont to do. Jones affected a lack of interest in whether some of his congregation wanted to leave with Leo Ryan, insisting that anybody was free to come and go as they pleased. When the number of those who wanted to return to the United States swelled to 15, however, Jones realized that his dream was under serious threat. Those 15 defectors would undoubtedly tell the truth about Jonestown, and once that truth was known even Jim Jones would not be able to explain away the catalogue of abuse. With no one to hold him to account, the cult leader had turned Jonestown into his personal kingdom; the loft at his parent's home writ large.

Jim Jones's voice broadcast from loudspeakers around the compound for hours on end, day and night. Sometimes he would deliver sermons live, but when he was indisposed tapes of pre-recorded speeches would be played. To maintain control he sent undercover informants out to test the loyalty of their fellow cult members. If any were found to be disloyal they would be 'treated' with electro-shock therapy until they fell back into line. Adults and children alike were forced to compete in boxing matches, and beaten with wooden paddles for even minor transgressions of the compound's numerous rules.

Children were beaten and microphones held to their mouths as they screamed so that everyone could hear the punishments. Jones would organize rehearsals of mass suicides, called 'white nights', when he would order the cult members to drink potions that he said contained poison. He constantly warned them that the time was coming when the compound would be raided, and that they needed to be ready to die at any moment. That alone would guarantee their passage to the new planet he believed was their true home.

While they waited for that time to come, the cult members were worked relentlessly, toiling for hours in the fields to grow enough food to live on. Their rations of rice and beans were meagre: Jim Jones dined separately on meat kept in his personal refrigerator, claiming he had problems with his blood-sugar levels. His drinking and drug-taking were harder to hide from his congregation in the small compound, and once the cult members saw the true Jim Jones many of them lost faith in the utopian experiment. The visit of Leo Ryan offered them their only chance of escape.

Suicide mission

The congressman gathered up those who wanted to leave and took them with him to the airport. On the way out of the compound, Temple member Don Sly suddenly lunged at him with a knife. Ryan was slashed but escaped, bleeding, with the 15 members who sought to return home. The Ryan party left at speed, but were pursued by members of Jim Jones's personal army, the Red Brigade. At the airport, this band of paramilitaries opened fire on the defectors with pistols, rifles and shotguns: 11 people were wounded as they fled for cover, and five were killed. One of those slain was congressman Leo Ryan – to date the only sitting member of the US House of Representatives to have been assassinated in office. Wounded by more than 20 bullets in the initial hail of gunfire, Ryan was finished off by a shotgun blast to the head at point-blank range.

Jones, who ordered the hit, broke the news to his congregation at an emergency meeting back at the compound. It seems he originally planned to have his men launch a suicide mission against the pilot of the Cessna aircraft while it was in the air. However two planes were needed to transport all those who wanted to leave Jonestown, so the assassination had to take place on the ground instead. The psychopath was determined to leave a record of the historic events for posterity, and as a result we know exactly what he said in the hours that followed. A tape recorder found later reveals how Jones persuaded more than 900 people to kill themselves and one another in the most extraordinary act of mass suicide–murder ever seen.

'Lay down your life with dignity,' says Jones on the tape recording. 'Don't lay down with tears and agony ... I don't care how many screams you hear; death is a million times preferable to spend more days in this life ... Have trust. You have to step across. This world was not our home.'

Some cult members are heard remonstrating that they want to live, or at least spare the lives of their children, but they are shouted down. A ring of heavily armed guards ensured that none could flee the scene. One by one the congregation stepped forward to drink the cyanide-laced Flavor-Aid drink. It was later incorrectly described as Kool-Aid and to this day 'drinking the Kool-Aid' has become shorthand for blindly following irrational orders. Many of those who refused to drink were injected with poison anyway, or shot as they ran away. By the time the grim procession was over, 912 people were dead, 276 of them children. And then the grand egotist himself joined them. Not by taking poison: Jim Jones was the Special One and had to remain so even in death. He shot himself in the head with a pistol.

The world, and the United States in particular, was horrified. All those in power who had supported Jones now rushed to distance themselves from him as his true psychopathic nature became clear. The state of Delaware even passed legislature stating that none of the Jonestown dead could be buried or cremated in the state. The Dover Air Force Base there is the US government's mortuary of choice, handling war dead for decades and used also in the aftermath of the September 11 attacks. Jones's body was secretly taken to Eglington, New Jersey, and cremated there before his ashes were scattered at sea. Everybody was anxious to ensure there was no lasting shrine to the insane cult leader.

None of the mass suicide cults since Jim Jones – and there have been many – has resulted in such a devastating loss of life. The events at Waco, Texas, resulted in 82 members of the Branch Davidian sect losing their lives, and large numbers killed themselves due to their membership of the Aum Shinrikyo, Order of the Solar Temple and Heaven's Gate cults. But it is the phrase 'Another Jonestown' that still strikes terror into anyone with relatives trapped under the influence of a cult. In that way the ghost of the psychopath Jim Jones still haunts the world, granting him a grim immortality in which he would no doubt revel.

Depictions such as this portrayed Blackbeard as
a fearsome adversary.

CHAPTER 8

BLACKBEARD

We'll probably never know the real name of Blackbeard, the psychopathic pirate who terrorized the Caribbean seas in the 18th century. Pirates of this period often used fictitious names in order to protect the good name of their real family, and the early records of Blackbeard's life are sparse. We first encounter him under the name Edward Teach, but often Thatch, Thack and other variations of the name are used. They may be different men: all we can surmise is that he was born sometime around 1680, and probably somewhere close to Bristol in the West of England. The city was an important international seaport at the time, and on the back of the wealth generated by the slave trade it rose to become, briefly, the second largest city in England. Teach must have learnt to read and write at some point, and was therefore probably not from a poor background. It is highly likely that he was born to a family of wealth and privilege – though whether that wealth brought respectability, too, will never be known. Was he thrown out in disgrace, or did he venture out to sea voluntarily in search of adventure? We can only speculate from the facts we know of his later life. He certainly had a voracious sexual appetite, later marrying no fewer than 14 wives. He had a quick and violent temper, and it seems improbable that this combination sat easily with the upper-class English etiquette of the period.

Hornigold's crew

The next time we sight Teach he is already at sea, probably working as a low-rank sailor operating out of Jamaica. He may well have signed up (or been abducted from a bar, as was common) to fight in Queen Anne's War. The struggle for control of North America between the French and the English began in 1702 and raged for more than a decade. Privateers were not only tolerated but actively encouraged by the Crown and it may be on one such ship that the young Blackbeard learnt the ropes of armed conflict at sea and on land. The war was marked by a series of bloody raids that drew the Native American tribes into the conflict, and both European powers were astonished and terrified by the ferocity of their fighting style. It may be that Blackbeard witnessed the brutal close-quarters combat at first hand, and learnt from it.

What's certain is that by the time the war ended in 1713, Blackbeard was working as a crewman for the pirate Benjamin Hornigold. He was placed in charge of his own sloop, and soon he was joining Hornigold in attacks on shipping. Initially the pirates hit smaller, undefended cargo ships carrying flour, spices and wine. Though not so alluring as gold or silver, these goods were still very valuable in the 18th century. We have few accounts of how Blackbeard operated at this time, but we do know that by 1717 he was noteworthy enough to merit a mention from Captain Matthew Munthe, a Navy man who patrolled the seas off North Carolina. Teach was getting a reputation as a menace to honest seafarers, but he was yet to transform himself into the legend we know today.

Had he continued to target small cargo ships, there is little doubt that he could have lived comfortably and with little danger of being captured. The psychopath, however, is drawn to ever-greater risk and ever-greater danger. In 1717 Teach was given control of a new craft, commandeered from a fellow-pirate whose crew of 70 had grown dissatisfied with their captain. Teach was by now well-known as a man who could deliver great riches to his crews, so they gladly followed him.

Blackbeard's timing was perfect: the early eigtheenth century marked the beginning of truly global trade, and the Florida Strait shipping lanes were teeming with ships taking valuable cargo back and forth between the New World and the Old. The remote harbours in which the pirate ships moored were too shallow for the Royal Navy's larger vessels to navigate and the vast expanses of open ocean gave outlaws plenty of places to flee to should they be intercepted during an attack. Blackbeard, like many other pirates at the time, settled on the then largely uninhabited island of New Providence in the Bahamas. It was inevitable that he would not remain Hornigold's underling for long, and the two soon argued over whether to limit themselves to attacking only the ships that belonged to England's enemies or to plunder any ship they came across. Blackbeard won the day and Hornigold was forced to retire. In total control of a fleet of pirate ships, Blackbeard was now free to do entirely as he pleased. It is when he has total control that a psychopath is both at his happiest and at his most dangerous.

Terror of the seas

Teach immediately became more daring and more vicious. In November 1717 his two ships blasted apart a small fleet of French merchant vessels, killing several French crewmen. The pirates took command of the ships, offloaded the cargo and used the money from the crime to equip their ships with ferocious new firepower. The largest stolen ship, *La Concorde*, was refitted with 40 large cannon and renamed *Queen Anne's Revenge*. It was to become the most feared pirate ship in history. Though Blackbeard's reign as the undisputed King of the Pirates was brief, it was also sensationally successful, and he would write his name in the history books as the most ferocious sea-warrior the world has ever seen. The secrets of his success were his daring, his unpredictability and his willingness to use extreme force to get whatever he wanted – all classic signs of a psychopathic personality.

The new pirate ships brought their terrible firepower to bear first on the merchant ship *Great Allen* just a few days after setting out to sea. She was a well-armed vessel and put up fierce resistance, but was over-whelmed by the *Queen Anne's Revenge*. Blackbeard was angered at being forced to fight for what he believed was rightfully his to take, so to send a message to other vessels he ordered the *Great Allen* be run aground and then burnt. It was an early act of terrorism, designed to cow any future ships' captains and dissuade them from resisting when attacked by his fleet. Blackbeard was, like many psychopaths, a master of psychological warfare. His appearance was deliberately cultivated to instil fear in those he encountered. It was described in detail by the writer Charles Johnson in his 1724 book *A General History of the Robberies and Murders of the most notorious Pyrates*:

'Captain Teach assumed the cognomen of Blackbeard from that large quantity of hair, which, like a frightful meteor, covered his whole face, and frightened America more than any comet that has appeared there a long time. This beard was black, which he suffered to grow of an extravagant length; as to breadth, it came up to his eyes; he was accustomed to twist it with ribbons, in small tails ... and turn them about his ears.'

The extravagant beard was reported to be set off with flaming matches or torches entwined within it, with further flames burning beneath the rim of his wide hat. He wore fine silk clothes over which he strapped a bandolier containing six pistols. The flag he flew from his ship's mast depicted a skeleton piercing a heart with a spear while raising a toast to the devil. The earliest illustrations of him generally show him brandishing a large cutlass, which he was said to wield with astonishing speed in hand-to-hand combat. There was precious little of that in the years that followed, however: Blackbeard's campaign of terror had the desired effect and the vast majority of vessels he attacked gave in to his demands without resisting.

The notorious pirate increased his personal wealth and fleet size at prodigious speed throughout the next two years. Other pirates preferred to select targets that would not draw the wrath of the most powerful navy on earth, the British

Royal Navy, but Blackbeard was utterly unconcerned about such matters. It is common for psychopaths to believe that they are beyond the laws that govern mere mortals, and Blackbeard was no different in this regard. The merchants, however, vigorously petitioned the authorities to take action against Blackbeard before his own fleet rivalled the navy's in power.

Ruthless ambition

In 1718, this seemed a real possibility: there was no limit to Blackbeard's ambition, and through sheer force of will and ruthless piracy he had amassed a fleet of astonishing power. In May 1718 he announced that he had promoted himself to the title of Commodore, and embarked on his most ambitious plan yet. He used his fleet to blockade the port of Charles Town (today known as Charleston) in South Carolina. Every single ship entering or leaving the port was stopped and ransacked. Blackbeard showed no regard for the social standing or influence of those who were on board the vessels: one prisoner taken was a member of the Council of the Province of Carolina, and many others were highly prominent members of the Charleston elite. To Blackbeard they were merely bargaining chips for him to use to get what he wanted. In this case he demanded the colonial government of South Carolina hand over all of their medical supplies, because many of his crew were suffering from disease. He threatened to execute his prisoners one by one until his demands were met. The governor was told that if he did not comply he would be sent the severed heads of the prisoners, and that every ship in the harbour would then be burnt. He paid up. The prisoners were released, albeit after they had been relieved of all their valuables.

Blackbeard then moved his fleet to North Carolina. After running aground, he sent ashore one of his co-conspirators, Stede Bonnet, to sound out the local governor about the possibility of being granted a pardon for his prior crimes. At the time, an amnesty was available to pirates who renounced their ways, so long as they surrendered before the deadline of 5 September 1718. As soon as his envoy left, Blackbeard stripped Bonnet's ship of everything of value and marooned its crew. Psychopaths do not believe in trust or loyalty: though they fully understand the value of the concept, they treat the trust of others as a weakness to exploit. Bonnet was desperate for revenge, but never managed to track down the wily Blackbeard, and he and his crew were hanged after returning to piracy shortly afterwards. It is highly likely that the entire 'accident' of running the ships aground was a cynical ploy by Blackbeard to reduce his fleet's size in order to keep more of the spoils for himself.

More men were marooned on a small island in the

Ocracoke Inlet, probably because they failed to show sufficient respect to their tyrannical captain. Marooning men on islands with no means of escape was a common punishment among pirates, and was almost always a death sentence. Blackbeard was known to be a very severe taskmaster, who had no sentimentality regarding even his most faithful and longest-serving crewmembers. The slightest transgression could be punished with lashings, maimings or death. This detached lack of empathy and inability to form emotional bonds with others is the hallmark of the psychopath, and Blackbeard provides us with a classic example.

Lure of the outlaw life

Deceit and lies are of no consequence to the psychopath, and shortly after betraying Bonnet, Blackbeard moved to obtain a pardon for his crimes from Governor Eden in nearby Bath Creek. With this in his pocket, he then obtained a commission as a privateer, to give his operation a veneer of respectability. Privateers were essentially mercenaries who did the Crown's dirty work at sea, attacking hostile ships but leaving alone the English vessels. Blackbeard, however, had no intention of abiding by any such rules and regulations and within a month a warrant was issued for his arrest on further charges of piracy. The renegade pirate had once again eschewed the chance to live safely and within the law in favour of an outlaw life of risk and adventure. It was, in the end, this risk and adventure that he lived for, not the wealth that his crimes brought him.

HMS *Pearl*

By now Blackbeard had a vast price on his head: not just a reward from the Crown, but an additional one from the Assembly of Virginia, whose members were terrified when they learnt of Blackbeard's presence off their shoreline. The reward rose further when the Assembly was informed that Blackbeard had teamed up with fellow pirate Charles Vane. Vane had risen to infamy by escaping from a fleet of Royal Navy ships by loading his own ships with explosives, setting fire to them and then letting them drift into the navy fleet. Also partying with Blackbeard were seasoned buccaneer Edward England and 'Calico Jack' Rackham. With such a fearsome band of pirates in the vicinity, Governor Alexander Spotswood turned to Royal Navy lieutenant Robert Maynard for help, placing at his disposal two converted merchant sloops, *Ranger* and *Jane*, to complement the 42-gun Navy gunboat Maynard sailed, HMS *Pearl*.

Maynard was in many ways the polar opposite of Blackbeard: methodical, logical and possessed of a calm determination to do his duty. He studied the geography of Blackbeard's last known location, information passed to him thanks to the treachery of a captured member of Blackbeard's crew. He stopped all traffic heading into or out of the inlet where Blackbeard was moored, to prevent any word of his presence from reaching the pirate. Lookouts were posted to ensure no escape could be made out to sea, and soundings were taken to determine the depth of the channels into the inlet.

In marked contrast, no lookouts were posted on board Blackbeard's ship: the pirate was hosting a lavish drunken party and was caught utterly unaware. The sense of invincibility that a psychopath often feels is very frequently the ultimate cause of their downfall, and so it would prove with Blackbeard.

The fight was brief but ferocious, rather like Blackbeard's life. Although in a seemingly hopeless situation, Blackbeard chose not to surrender to the navy ships that surrounded him. He would not be taken alive.

As soon as he spotted Maynard's main vessels approaching, Blackbeard blasted away with all the guns available on his ship *Adventure*. As the damaged sloops retreated, Blackbeard cut his anchor and chased them down, raining down ferocious fire. Though the navy was aware of the awesome firepower at Blackbeard's disposal, experiencing it first-hand was an altogether different matter and for a while it looked as though the navy would be defeated. As many as 30 Royal Navy sailors lay dead and both of their sloops were badly damaged. Rather than escaping out to sea or across land, however, Blackbeard again showed his daring personality by attempting to board the damaged navy sloops. He threw primitive grenades made from gunpowder and shot onto the decks, then hurled out grappling hooks and climbed aboard, pistol drawn.

Fight to the death ...

Maynard remained icily calm. He had ordered the bulk of his uninjured men to stay below deck, and he then waited patiently for the legendary pirate to walk into his trap. Once Blackbeard was on board, Maynard's men burst forth onto the decks and engaged the pirates with pistols and swords. According to historical records, the two men faced one another in the midst of the fighting. Blackbeard told Maynard that he would show him no mercy nor expect any in return, and Maynard replied that he had expected nothing more nor less. As Blackbeard lunged towards Maynard, he was gunned down and slashed apart by Royal Navy sailors. His body was later discovered to have five bullet wounds and 20 cuts upon it. Maynard ordered Blackbeard's head to be severed, and he hung it from the bowsprit of his ship during the triumphant return journey to North Carolina. Blackbeard's remaining crew were captured, tried and executed.

But his name lives on ...

Unexplained lights at sea are even today referred to by sailors as 'Teach's light' and said to be the ghost of Blackbeard, in search of his severed head. Though other pirates were more successful in terms of the bounty they looted, or the length of time they reigned, none lives on so brightly as Blackbeard.

That legendary status is testimony to the astonishing power of the terrifying image he so carefully cultivated during his lifetime. The truth behind the legend is scarcely any less terrifying: Blackbeard was a charismatic psychopath devoid of fear or pity. These terrible human failings made him the perfect pirate.

The capture of Blackbeard as imagined
by Jean Léon Gérome Ferris in 1718.

A still captured from CC-TV footage of Eric Harris (left) and Dylan Kiebold at Columbine High School.

CHAPTER 9

ERIC HARRIS

In the basement bedroom at 8276 South Reed St, in suburban Littleton, Colorado, two teenagers met every evening to discuss their dreams of the future. They both shared the same ambition: to become not sports stars or rock stars, but the most infamous murderers in history. Their vision of the future was apocalyptic. First, massive bombs would tear apart their school, blowing open the bodies of hundreds of their fellow-students. Then the terrified survivors would be gunned down with automatic weapons as they fled. Finally, as the police, rescue services and world's media gathered in the car park, car bombs would explode to wreak further devastation live on television. After the carnage, the United States would never be the same again, and the names of the perpetrators would live on forever in infamy.

Posterity has a few miswired devices to thank for the

fact that their vision was not fully realized: the bombs failed to detonate. But the teenagers' Plan B was horrific enough to ensure they would indeed go down in history as two of the most savage mass murderers ever to attack on American soil. The young men in question were Eric Harris and Dylan Klebold, and the attack they carried out on 20 April 1999 is usually summarized today in a single word: Columbine.

Eric Harris and Dylan Klebold acted together but were very different individuals. Klebold's personality type is one horribly familiar to those who study school shootings: an angry outsider, impulsive, depressive and suicidal. But Eric Harris was far more unusual. Everyone who knew him described him as well-spoken, intelligent and, above all, 'nice'. When the FBI asked some of the world's best mental health experts to look at the case so that they could learn lessons from it, the psychiatrists' verdict on Harris was chilling. Beneath the 'nice' veneer of the 'normal kid' from Wichita lurked a cold-blooded psychopath.

No childhood trauma

Most psychopaths have troubled childhoods, and show signs of psychological abnormality early on. Eric Harris appears to be one of the rare exceptions. He was born in Wichita, Kansas, on 9 April 1981. His father Wayne was in the US Air Force and his mother Kathy was a homemaker. Wayne's career meant he was posted to several different bases, which meant the family moved around a great deal. Eric attended elementary school in Oscoda, Michigan, where his parents went to every school conference and were told by teachers that their two children (Eric had an older brother, Kevin) were doing well. When the Wurtsmith Air Force Base in Oscoda began to be wound down in 1991 and most staff left, the Harris family uprooted to Plattsburgh, New York, where again they appeared to be a normal, happy family. Neighbours remember the boys attending Scouts and playing Little League baseball. In 1993 they moved again, this time back to Wayne and Kathy's home state of Colorado. They rented and then bought a home in Littleton, and Eric began to attend Ken Caryl Middle School. In the seventh or eighth grade he met Dylan Klebold. The two rapidly became inseparable. It was a relationship that would last for the rest of their short lives.

Gifted but socially isolated

Dylan Bennet Klebold was the son of a geophysicist and a counsellor who attended a Lutheran church and observed Jewish rituals at home. He was brought up in a house without guns: even toy guns were banned from the family home. That home was an imposing building in Deer Creek

Canyon whicht Eric would jokingly refer to as his 'country house'. Dylan's bedroom was on the second floor and he spent much of his time there playing computer games. Both he and Harris were early adopters of computer technology and were considered geeks by the rest of their class. 'Doom' was a particular favourite of theirs, and Harris wrote and distributed his own bespoke levels for the game.

Dylan's intellectual promise had resulted in him being enrolled in the Challenging High Intellectual Potential Students (CHIPS) program for gifted children at elementary school. But while mentally brilliant he was emotionally awkward. Klebold was lanky, quiet and shy, in contrast to Harris who was sarcastic and loud. The two outsiders bonded and found solace in one another's company. Klebold called himself Vodka, after his favourite drink, while Harris answered to Reb, short for 'rebel'. Harris' profile on WBS (Web Broadcasting System, an early type of chat forum) read: 'I kill who I don't like, I waste what I don't want, I destroy what I hate.' It might well serve as a summary for the world-view of all psychopaths.

During his freshman year, Eric took a girl called Tiffany Typher to the homecoming, but she refused to go out with him on another date. He responded by staging a fake suicide, sprawling on the ground with fake blood all over his body. Though he dismissed it as a joke, it was in reality a sign of the kind of vindictive psychological manipulation in which Harris was by now skilled. In the same year he wrote in a classmate's yearbook 'Ich bin Gott', meaning 'I am God' in German. Both Harris and Klebold were fascinated by German rock bands and Nazi history. They were both bullied mercilessly by the sporty 'jocks' from the year above them: in one incident Klebold was pelted with ketchup-covered tampons. Harris suffered from a mild physical defect, having been born with a slight indentation in his chest. It made him reluctant to take off his shirt in gym class, and he felt physically inferior to his taller, more bulky older brother.

Imagined acts of revenge

Harris and Klebold increasingly withdrew into the fantasy world they shared, in which they imagined avenging themselves on their tormentors, and on a society they judged to be superficial and hypocritical. Eric changed his hairstyle from a flattop to spiky and began to wear a trench coat rather than a preppy jacket. His parents' hope that he would follow his older brother into college were dashed when he announced that he planned instead to join the US Marines.

Eric followed Dylan's example by getting a job at a local pizza parlour. They spent much of their earnings on fireworks, which they set off in alleys and in fields, binding the devices together to create ever more powerful explosions. Eric set a fire in the sink of the pizza parlour's kitchen. The fascination with arson and explosions is one that is seen time and time again in the psychopathic mind. The control, fear and excitement are all ingredients that the psychopath tends to enjoy. Often arson is the precursor to more extreme acts of violence, and so it would prove in the case of Eric Harris.

Initially Harris engaged in only low-level acts of intimidation against those he perceived to have wronged him. A schoolmate who was late giving him a ride suffered a campaign of terror at Harris' hands. Eric posted the name of the boy, Brooks Brown, online, along with his home address and phone number. He placed firecrackers in Brown's mailbox and broke his car windscreen. When the Brown family complained, Eric's father Wayne began to take notice of his errant son's actions and record his behaviour in a journal. The police were informed but took no further action, convinced it was simply a case of a petty teenage rivalry. Harris intimidated other classmates with similar low-level harassment, and kept detailed logs of his 'missions', which he posted online. The logs show that though Harris complained about the bullying of others, he was himself a bully of the very worst kind. Of one victim he wrote: 'Everyone in our school hates this immature little weakling', while going on to describe attacking his house with eggs, toilet rolls, fireworks and superglue. It was still typical childish stuff, but the desire for vengeance was very real and would soon escalate to truly deadly levels.

It was in January 1998 that Eric and Dylan first came to the attention of the police for a serious matter. They were caught after breaking into a van and stealing some electronic equipment. Both were sentenced to community service, and ordered to attend rehabilitation classes. Eric's mother also took him to see an anger-management therapist. He was prescribed antidepressants, chiefly Luvox, which some would later suggest only made his mood worse. Taking the drugs also ended his hopes of joining the Marines – though he would discover this only much later.

'I lie a lot'

Though the crime Harris and Klebold were convicted of was relatively minor, their reactions to being caught are illuminating. Klebold confessed immediately, but Harris protested his innocence, claiming that it was his friend's idea, and that he just happened to be present at the time. His lack of remorse and inability to take personal responsibility is evident in his journal writings of the time. There he rants about how he ought to be entitled to take things from those who are stupid enough to leave them in a van. 'Isn't America supposed to be the land of the free?' asked Harris, arguing that he should be free to 'deprive' his victim of their goods if they are foolish enough to leave them on display.

That sense of entitlement is a key character-trait in psychopaths, and a second key trait is duplicity. In this, too, Harris excelled: he claimed to be genuinely sorry and wrote long essays explaining how anger management had helped him to see the error of his ways. In private he continued to gloat about his crimes, and rail against the injustice of society in holding him to account for them. His school principal later remarked that Harris was the kind of person who told those in authority what they wanted to hear. It was only after the tragic events at Columbine High School that they realized who Harris really was. His journals and web postings make it crystal clear that the often charming Eric Harris was an inveterate liar. 'I lie a lot,' he admitted in his journal. 'Almost constantly, and to everybody, just to keep my own ass out of the water. Let's see, what are some of the big lies I told? Yeah I stopped smoking. For doing it, not for getting caught. No I haven't been making more bombs. No I wouldn't do that. And countless other ones.'

The lies Harris told were not simply to 'keep my own ass out of the water', but for the pure pleasure of fooling people. To psychopaths, persuading another person to believe something untrue is a sign of superiority. It delights psychopaths to know something that other people do not, even if what they know is only what brilliant liars they are. Harris's duplicity was the key factor that allowed the Columbine massacre to become a moment of hideous reality rather than remaining a twisted fantasy. 'God I can't wait till I can kill you people,' wrote Harris. 'I'll just go to some downtown area is some big ass city and blow up and shoot everything I can. Feel no remorse, no sense of shame.'

Preparations for cold-blooded slaughter

That seething rage against the world in general soon coalesced into a concrete and specific plan to attack those closest to him: his classmates at Columbine High. He and Klebold planned the events of that day in meticulous detail, for over a year. They assembled the arsenal of weapons they would need and carefully scoped the school for the areas where they could cause maximum mayhem and injury.

Their jobs at Blackjack Pizza provided not only the money required for purchasing weapons, but also access to the weapons themselves. A colleague there agreed to purchase two shotguns and a rifle for them, along with ammunition. The two practised firing them in nearby woods, using bowling pins and pine trees as target practice. They sawed the shotgun barrels down in order to better disguise them.

Meanwhile they also practised building primitive pipe bombs, using designs found on the Internet and whatever materials they could obtain. The early experiments with fireworks strapped together evolved into more sophisticated devices that better concentrated the blast. Through trial and error they improved their bombs, all the while seeking with chilling detachment to cause the maximum damage to as many human bodies as possible. Harris gave the bombs pet names and was elated when they were finished, writing 'Atlanta, Pholus, Peltro and Pazzie are complete. For those of you that don't know who they are, they are the first 4 true pipe bombs created entirely from scratch by the rebels (REB and VoDkA)'.

The two made videos in which they acted out violent fantasies and spoke directly of their plans for slaughter. In the fictional *Hitmen for Hire* Eric and Dylan run around in black trench coats wearing sunglasses, heroically wreaking vengeance on bullies on behalf of their victims. In the so-called *Basement Tapes* the two take it in turns to video one another speaking directly to camera. Harris calls his sawn-off shotgun Arlene and identifies another weapon as a carbine before boasting of how they are also creating homemade napalm and grenades. He states, 'It's a weird feeling knowing you're going to be dead in two and a half weeks.' Eric suggests that their story should be made into a film, and the two debate whether Steven

Spielberg or Quentin Tarantino should direct it. Many psychopaths live their lives in this detached way, as if they were the stars of a film rather than 'extras' in the vast sea of humanity. The world revolves around them and them alone. There is yet more evidence of Harris's extraordinarily grandiose sense of self when he turns the camera onto his journal, which he describes as 'The Writings of God'.

Bad, not mad

In another significant segment, Harris self-pityingly discusses the effect his actions will have on his parents. 'I wish I was a f***ing sociopath so I didn't have any remorse, but I do,' he says. 'This is going to tear them apart. They will never forget it.' It is a profound irony that Harris believes he has remorse, even before he commits the action he wants his audience to imagine he is sorry for. What he means is that he knows in advance that the action is wrong, and that it will hurt many people very deeply – but he is going to do it anyway. Psychopaths are not psychotic, nor are they criminally insane. They do not hear voices, or fail to understand the difference between right and wrong. They are, in the popular parlance, bad rather than mad. They speak, just as Harris does, of being 'destined' for certain things in life, and believe their lives are of such cosmic importance that they simply have to act in a particular way, even if their actions bring horror and pain to others.

The final tape the two made was on the morning of 20 April 1999 – just half an hour or so before leaving the Harris family home to launch their murderous attack on their classmates at Columbine High School. The majority of the so-called *Basement* Tapes were first embargoed and then destroyed, for fear of inspiring copy-cat killers. What we do know, in tragic detail, is what happened when the pair turned off the camera and drove, in separate cars, to the school that morning.

School massacre

Harris arrived first, in his grey Honda Civic, at around 11.10 a.m. Shortly afterwards Klebold's black BMW rolled up and parked, as per the plan, in a spot on the opposite side of the school cafeteria. Harris bumped into Brooks Brown, the student he had feuded with previously, and told him to go home as he 'liked him now'. Moments later, Harris and Klebold walked into the school cafeteria carrying duffel bags packed with explosive powder and propane. The crude bombs were timed to go off at 11.17 a.m., the time Harris had determined would result in the largest number of injuries. The bombs were placed on the floor beside two of the lunch tables, and then Harris and Klebold retreated back into their respective cars in the parking lot to wait for the devices to explode. Their plan was to shoot the survivors as they fled from the ensuing carnage.

At 11.19, Jefferson County Dispatch Center received the first 911 call of a bomb exploding, just as Harris had planned. The two murderers had placed a device in a field 5 kilometres south-west of Columbine High School. This was done purely to tie up fire, ambulance and police services so that they would be delayed in responding to the incident at the school. It worked: emergency services rushed to the field to deal with the major grass fire that had resulted from the explosion. The bombs planted at Columbine, thankfully, were less successful. After waiting in vain for them to blow apart the school, Harris took control of the situation and entered the building, urging Klebold on with the command 'Go! Go!' The two killers entered the building at 11.19 and began firing.

The first shots, fired towards the west doors, killed 17-year-old Rachel Scott and injured Richard Castaldo, also 17, who had been sitting on the grass eating their school lunch outside the school's entrance near the north side of the library. Three more students who were en route to the 'Smoker's Pit' were hit shortly afterwards, then another five sitting on the grass were gunned down. By now the sound of gunfire had caused the students in the cafeteria to flee in panic. One witness later reported hearing one of the gunmen shout, 'This is what we always wanted to do. This is awesome!' Harris ditched his trench coat and sent Klebold to check on the cafeteria bombs, both of the killers firing indiscriminately at any unfortunate classmates they encountered. Lance Kirklin pleaded for help as he lay mortally wounded at Klebold's feet. The gunman responded by saying: 'Sure, I'll help you' and then shot the 16-year-old in the face.

The pair threw pipe bombs towards larger pockets of students, though thankfully most failed to fully detonate. Art teacher Patti Nelson was hit by shrapnel as she walked towards the West Entrance to tell the students to 'knock it off'. She shepherded the terrified youngsters into the library and dialled 911. By the time the call was received the police had already begun to trade fire with Harris and Klebold. A deputy on duty at the school encountered the pair at 11.24, when Harris opened fire on his patrol car in the parking lot. Deputy Neil Gardner fired back with his service weapon and radioed for back-up: he was massively outgunned, and not wearing his prescription glasses. Just two minutes later the first back-up vehicle arrived and another shoot-out with Harris occurred. His ferocious fire was enough to tie down the officers and dissuade them from entering the building, which bought him time to continue his murderous rampage inside the school.

William 'Dave' Sanders was a computer and business teacher at Columbine and coach of the girls' basketball and softball teams. Harris shot him twice in the chest as he evacuated students from the cafeteria. Sanders made it to the science classroom with the help of another teacher, who placed a sign in the window to alert the authorities to the situation. It read: '1 bleeding to death'. Meanwhile, Patti Nelson cowered with 55 other teachers, students and librarians under desks in the library. The recording of her call to the police clearly captured the sound of Harris entering at 11.29 and shouting 'Get up!' When nobody responded to his order, Harris announced 'Fine, I'll start shooting anyway.' The ensuing massacre demonstrated the cold-blooded mercilessness that characterizes the true psychopath. Harris told 17-year-old Kacey Ruegsegger to 'quit your bitching' as she moaned in pain after being shot, and played a taunting game of 'Peek-a-boo' with 17-year-old Cassie Bernall before killing her with a shot to the back of the head. He racially abused 18-year-old Isaiah Shoels before firing a fatal shot into his chest, then roared: 'Who's ready to die next?', and threw a pipe bomb under another table. Both shooters regularly paused calmly to reload their weapons, and moved through the library murdering any student who took their eye. Some were spared, perhaps due to sheer indifference or because the killers were actively targeting the most sporty and popular of their peers. The most likely explanation is that the pair were simply growing bored with their own slaughter: several witnesses heard Harris complain that it was no longer thrilling to kill. The psychopath grows bored easily. Klebold suggested they begin stabbing their victims instead, and Harris tossed a Molotov cocktail to try and bring some variety to the live horror show. And then they left the library, leaving 10 dead, 12 wounded and 34 unharmed.

The pair were by now running out of exciting targets, and running out of time. They drifted through the science area, throwing firebombs and shooting aimlessly, then headed back down to the cafeteria, where Harris tried desperately to detonate the failed bombs by firing directly at them. Klebold eventually managed to persuade one of the propane bombs to partially explode by throwing a Molotov cocktail at it. The resulting fire was soon extinguished by the school's automatic fire sprinklers. Through the windows the two could see the police swarming over the scene, and they fired several rounds in their direction, but did not hit anyone. The psychopath craves excitement and control, and Harris was by now losing both. He and Klebold returned to the library for the final scene of their drama. At around 12.08 they shouted 'One! Two! Three!' in unison, and committed suicide. Klebold shot himself in the left temple with his

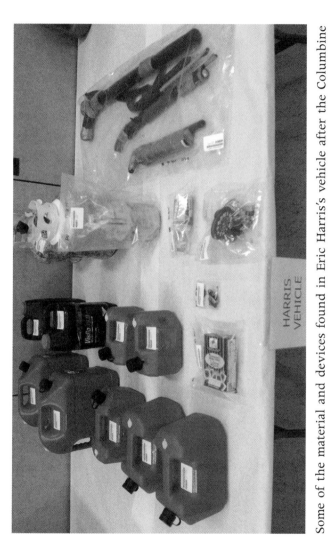

Some of the material and devices found in Eric Harris's vehicle after the Columbine High School massacre.

TEC-9 semi-automatic handgun; Harris placed his sawn-off shotgun into his mouth and pulled the trigger. SWAT teams entered the building at 1.09 p.m.: 12 students and one teacher lay dead or dying inside, and a further 21 were injured.

'Full of hate'

One of the last entries in Eric Harris's journal read: 'I hate you people for leaving me out of so many fun things ... you people had my phone number, and I asked and all, but no. No no no don't let the weird-looking Eric kid come along.' It provides his own insight into why he inflicted so much suffering upon his classmates. As far as Harris was concerned, they had it coming – it was no act of random murder but merely an act of social justice. Author Dave Cullen, who spent ten years researching a book on the Columbine tragedy, came to a different conclusion: Harris was a cold-blooded psychopath, who punished others for what he perceived to be their inferiority. Professor Aubrey Immelman suggested Harris was a paranoid narcissist with an uncontrollable aggressive streak. At a summit convened by the FBI to look at what could be learned from Columbine, psychiatrist Dr Frank Ochberg pointed to the toxic combination of the two shooters' personalities: Klebold was a depressive who was hurting inside, Harris was a psychopath who wanted to hurt others. The two made a deadly combination, with Klebold's fits of rage providing the deadly spark that Harris's calm and calculated psychopathy needed to burst into flame.

It should be remembered that, tragic as Columbine was, it was in the end only a small part of the killers' horrific master plan. They intended Columbine to be not the worst school shooting in American history, but the worst act of any kind of civilian slaughter. Had the bombs gone off as planned, the death toll would undoubtedly have been much, much higher. In an eerie pre-echo of the events of September 2001, Harris and Klebold even discussed plans to hijack a jet plane and crash it in to a building in New York. Others later dreamt the same dark dream, and turned it into a grim reality, but Harris was, in the end, too impatient to kill to ever properly implement such a grandiose scheme. He did not possess the brilliant mind he imagined himself to have. Though his actions defy rational explanation, what motivated those actions is the banal truth common to all psychopaths, which is the belief that they are better than those around them. In his journal, Harris himself summed it up like this: 'I'm full of hate and I love it.'

Ted Bundy acts up in the courtroom at the end of a session during his trial.

CHAPTER 10

TED BUNDY

While Theodore Robert Cowell didn't have the kind of stereotypically harsh upbringing of many serial killers, he didn't have it easy, either. He was born in Vermont in November 1946 to Eleanor Louise Cowell, who had become pregnant by a serviceman who was no longer on the scene. Louise had no option but to throw herself on the mercy of her parents and she moved in with them and her newborn boy in Philadelphia. Samuel and Eleanor Cowell were desperate to avoid their daughter's scandalous behaviour becoming the talk of the neighbourhood and so they pretended that Theodore was their son; Ted thus grew up believing his mother was in fact his sister. He didn't discover the truth until he was in his twenties, and for the rest of his life he bore a fierce resentment towards his mother for lying to him.

His relationship with his grandparents (who at the time

he believed were his parents) was complicated. Samuel Cowell was a tyrannical man who was bigoted against African-Americans, Roman Catholics and Jews. He was often violent towards his wife and cruel to neighbourhood animals: on more than one occasion he swung cats by their tails. Eleanor Cowell received electroconvulsive therapy for depression and gradually became afraid to leave the house. Ted later claimed that he was close to his grandparents, however, and held a respect for Samuel that never wavered.

Sexual obsessions

The tell-tale early psychopathic symptoms were present from an early age: when he was just three years old he took all of the knives from the kitchen and placed them around his sleeping 'sister' (actually his aunt) Julia. She woke to find her nephew grinning at her from the bottom of the bed. In 1950, Louise and Ted moved to Tacoma, Washington, where Louise's new partner, hospital cook Johnny Culpepper Bundy, formally adopted the young boy. Theodore Cowell became Ted Bundy. With a less strict regime to live under, Ted wandered the streets raiding rubbish bins for pictures of naked women, and became interested in detective stories and true crime books. From an early age he showed an unhealthy interest in sadomasochistic sex crimes, in particular. At school he got good grades but did not mix well with other children. Like most psychopaths, he developed a reputation for being a loner and an outsider.

Another key indicator of psychopathic behaviour was also present: Ted Bundy was frequently in trouble with the law. As a child and young adult his crimes were relatively minor – he was arrested twice on suspicion of burglary and auto theft before he turned 18. He also took to prowling around, peeking in through undrawn curtains to try to catch glimpses of naked bodies or couples having sex. Mostly he committed petty thefts of skiing equipment to support his interest in the past-time. To a psychopath, stealing represents their sense of entitlement – the entire world and everything in it belongs to them. What they want, they take, without shame or remorse. Psychopaths also tend to be relentless thrill-seekers – the buzz of stealing may well have been as important to Bundy as the actual articles he took.

He managed to get into college, attending the University of Puget Sound in Washington, and there his handsome features caught the eye of a young classmate with whom he became romantically involved. Her name is usually given as 'Stephanie Brooks' in order to protect her real identity (often the names of his victims are also changed, which is why differing accounts give a bewildering variety of victim names). Stephanie was to have the most profound and deadly impact upon the young man's life.

Restless and dishonest

Brooks was the kind of girl that Bundy had always dreamed of marrying: hugely attractive, intelligent and from an extremely wealthy Californian family. For a time he was deliriously happy, but Stephanie soon grew tired of his apparent lack of focus in life. This impulsive jumping from one area of interest to another is a further key indicator of a psychotic personality. It is very rare to find a psychopath who does not get bored easily, and Ted Bundy was a classic example of this. He began to focus on his studies only once Stephanie had broken off the relationship, and by then it was too late. His habit of lying in order to impress her backfired and she simply refused to believe he had truly changed.

Bundy dropped out of college altogether, then re-entered with renewed fervour and an almost obsessive interest in psychology. His personality shifted from intro-verted to confident and sociable. Again we can see the psychopathic traits in play: Bundy never understood how true social bonds worked, but while at college he suddenly learned how to fake such bonds convincingly. He posed as a supporter of former governor Albert Rosellini in order to gain information for Daniel J. Evans, his opponent in the election campaign. Working undercover allowed Bundy to hone his skills of deception and deceit – traits already well advanced in most psychopaths.

He began a relationship with a divorcée from Utah who worked as a secretary at the university. The woman is variously identified in Bundy accounts as Meg Anders, Beth Archer or Liz Kendall, but her real name is Elizabeth Kloepfer. Her tempestuous relationship with Bundy began in the autumn of 1969, during which time his behaviour would become increasingly bizarre and violent. Initially, however, he displayed the superficial charisma common to many psychopaths. Armed with his natural good looks and newfound charm, he now possessed all the tools he needed to act out the murderous fantasies he harboured in his mind. Shortly after midnight on 4 January 1974, his reign of terror began.

Murder spree

Karen Sparks's room-mates started to get concerned when she didn't surface from her basement bedroom on the morning of 4 January. When it got to mid-afternoon they went knocking and entered her room. They found the 18-year-old lying bloody, bruised and unconscious on her bed. Part of the bedframe had been ripped off and used as a weapon on her before she was sexually assaulted. She was rushed to hospital, where she remained in a coma for ten days. Although left permanently brain-damaged, the first of Bundy's documented victims was one of the few who survived.

Though nobody yet made the connection, Karen bore a striking physical similarity to the woman who had spurned Bundy, Stephanie Brooks. Though Bundy later denied there was ever any conscious connection between his victims and Stephanie, all wore their dark hair parted down the middle. It is not known precisely when he began killing, and the attack on Karen was almost certainly not his first act of predatory sexual violence. When pressed to confess to all of his crimes, however, Bundy repeatedly changed his story as to where and when he murdered. It is yet another classic trait of the psychopath to lie in such a manner, even when it would appear he had little to gain by doing so; he knew by then he would go to the electric chair.

His second known victim was attacked less than a month after the first: Bundy broke into the basement room of another undergraduate, Lynda Ann Healy. She was a psychology major, and her voice was familiar to thousands in the Washington area, as she reported on the skiing conditions for local radio every morning. Bundy beat her unconscious, then dressed her in blue jeans and a white blouse, neatly made her bed, and carried her off into the night. Her room-mate in the next door bedroom heard nothing until her alarm went off, as usual, at 5.30 a.m. On this morning, however, Lynda was not there to shut it off.

Killer on the loose

Female college students continued to disappear at the rate of about one a month throughout the spring and summer of 1974. Donna Gail Manson disappeared in March on her way to a jazz concert. Susan Elaine Rancourt vanished on her way to watch a movie in April. Roberta Kathleen Parks failed to show for a meeting with friends in the Oregon State Student Union café in May. The police had little to go on: the only thing the women had in common was that they were young, attractive female students with long hair parted down the middle. Brenda Carol Ball's disappearance from outside the Flame Tavern in Burien, Washington, provided an early clue. She had been seen talking to a young, brown-haired man with his arm in a sling. This chimed with earlier reports of a man with a broken arm asking for help to load books into his tan-coloured Volkswagen Beetle on the night of Susan Rancourt's disappearance. The investigators were not yet sure of it, but they had stumbled across Bundy's modus operandi.

Deception and manipulation are two of the most powerful weapons in the psychopath's arsenal. Bundy exemplified this, preying on the good nature of his victims and taking advantage of the kindness they instinctively showed to those more vulnerable than themselves. His standard trick of asking for help would perhaps not have worked on the tough, street-wise kids of an inner-city area – but it was lethal when deployed against the middle-class students in Washington. They had been brought up to help those in need, and Bundy made sure he appeared to be exactly that, with a prominent plaster cast on display on his supposedly broken arm. He was also handsome, articulate and well-dressed – the kind of young man who raised no alarm bells. Indeed, Bundy would generally make a point of appearing to struggle on his own before asking for help, as if he were embarrassed at his need for assistance. The young women would then leap to his aid – and to their doom.

University of Washington student Georgann Hawkins was the next to fall victim to Bundy's technique, in June, though by this time he was on crutches with a leg cast. Police combed the alleyway between her boyfriend's dormitory and the sorority house she was heading towards, but found nothing. Again, however, eye-witness reports mentioned a man with a brown Volkswagen Beetle asking for help. In July, Janice Ott was approached on the crowded beach at Lake Sammamish State Park, east of Seattle, by a man who asked for help unloading his sailboat. Four hours later 18-year-old Denise Naslund was given a similar story. Both were murdered – one in front of the other, according to some reports. Their bodies were found near a service road 3 kilometres east of where they were last seen. The bones of Georgann Hawkins were found at the same spot.

Into Utah

Most psychopaths require ever-more stimulation from their actions, leading to ever-escalating violence in the case of serial killers. Bundy was by now no longer satisfied with a single victim per night. In August 1974 he moved to Salt Lake City to study at the University of Utah Law School. He rapidly became angry and frustrated at his inability to understand the lessons there. His grandiose sense of his own intellectual ability suddenly collided with the crushing reality that he simply wasn't that smart. The result of such a revelation to most people would be disappointment, but to a psychopath the result is murderous rage. So it proved in the coming months, as Bundy killed with increasing frequency and sadism.

A post-mortem examination of the body of 17-year-old Melissa Smith showed that she may have been alive for up to seven days after her disappearance. Exactly what horrors she endured during that period we will never know, but when her naked body was found in mountains of Utah it showed evidence of violent assault, rape, sodomy and strangulation. Bundy later described shampooing the corpse's hair and applying make-up to her face. He treated the body of his next victim, Laura Ann Aime, also 17, the same way. The desire to possess and totally control is common among psychopaths, and as so often Bundy gives a classic example of it in his behaviour. First he destroys all that is beautiful about his young victims, and then he rebuilds their physical appearance in the image that pleases him.

Risk-taking is another aspect of the psychopath's personality, and despite a massive manhunt Bundy continued to operate in the same location, right in the middle of an intensive police operation. He made no attempt to alter his appearance or change his distinctive car. Carol DaRonch was abducted less than a mile away from the spot where Melissa Smith vanished, and just a few days later. This time Bundy posed as police officer Roseland and ordered her into his car. She escaped as he tried to handcuff her. Impersonating a figure of authority gives the psychopath the kind of respect they believe they inherently deserve but are usually denied. To some extent, devoid of genuine empathy for others, all psychopaths are impersonators of one kind or another: they learn to ape the actions of others, and pass themselves off as psychologically normal human beings by copying what others do.

In November Bundy's girlfriend Elizabeth Kloepfer read about the Salt Lake City cases. She had contacted the police previously to suggest Ted Bundy as a suspect, but now she contacted them again: it was just too much of a coincidence that women were being attacked in the exact area where Ted had relocated. He was called in to participate in a line-up, but the most reliable witness to date failed to pick him out, and he was released. The close brush with the law did little to slow down Bundy's murder spree: psychopaths tend to believe they are all-powerful and rarely consider the possibility they might get held to account for their actions. In 1975 Bundy struck again, though by now he was back in Salt Lake City and stalking the women of neighbouring Colorado.

Caryn Campbell's naked body was found next to a dirt road a month after she disappeared. The 23-year-old nurse had been killed by blows to the head by a blunt weapon, then her body had been slashed with a blade. Bundy then murdered 26-year-old ski instructor Julie Cunningham some 150 kilometres further north-east, in March. He revisited her strangled corpse several weeks later to gain a fix of sexual excitement between killings. Such gaps were few and far between: Denise Oliverson was killed the next month, and a month after that Lynette Culver disappeared from outside Alameda Junior High School in Idaho. She was just 12 years old. Bundy sexually assaulted and then drowned her. By the end of June he had murdered once more: this time student Susan Curtis was the victim. Her body, like that of Wilcox, Kent, Cunnigham, Culver and Oliverson, was never found.

Arrested and jailed

In August 1975 Bundy was baptized into The Church of Jesus Christ of the Latter-day Saints. It was not a search for redemption, but instead a cynical ploy to cloak himself with respectability and divert the increasing suspicion and mistrust of those around him. He was by now right at the top of investigators' list of possible suspects, but it was a chance encounter with a Highway Patrol man that finally led to his arrest. Bundy failed to pull over for a routine traffic stop, which led to the officer searching his car. A ski-mask, crowbar and handcuffs were among the items found. Bundy was pulled in for questioning but released due to a lack of evidence. He was placed under surveillance, however, and when he finally got rid of the incriminating Volkswagen Beetle by selling it the police impounded the car. They found hairs from Caryn Campbell's body inside, and Bundy was once again compelled to take part in a line-up. This time he was picked out by Carol DaRonch, and as a result was charged with kidnapping and assault.

The police still didn't have enough evidence to bring Bundy to trial for the murders, but he was found guilty of the kidnap charge in June 1976 and given a sentence of one to fifteen years. A few months later he was caught hiding in bushes in the prison yard with an 'escape kit' consisting of a road map, airline schedules and a social security card. Bundy clearly didn't think he belonged in prison, and was in no mood to do his time quietly. When charged with the murder of Caryn Campbell, he elected to act as his own attorney, and was thus excused wearing handcuffs or leg shackles in court. At a preliminary hearing in Pitkin County Courthouse, he escaped through a window in the law library and hiked south onto Aspen Mountain before the police roadblocks and search dogs could stop him. He was free for six days before police caught him weaving through traffic in a stolen car.

Second escape

A man with a lesser ego than Bundy might have called it quits at that point: he was back in jail but his trial was going well, from his point of view, as the case against him was weakened by much of the evidence being ruled inadmissible. There was a good chance he might be acquitted. But the psychopath is not a rational individual, and escape was Bundy's new obsession. He bought a hacksaw blade from a fellow inmate, cut a hole in the ceiling of his cell and crawled to freedom. Courtesy of a stolen car, a hitched ride and a flight to Chicago, Bundy was a free man by the time the prison authorities noticed he was gone on 31 December 1977. It was a stunningly audacious move, and Bundy's reckless gamble appeared to have paid off. But again it isn't in the psyche of the psychopath to quit while he is ahead. Ted Bundy, now calling himself Chris Hagen, was not the kind of man to keep a low profile.

Bundy hung out in local taverns, chatting to the locals and watching ball games as he moved from state to state. He travelled by train to Michigan and then stole a car and drove to Atlanta. From there he boarded a bus to Florida, where he supported himself by shoplifting and petty theft.

It was never going to be enough excitement for a man addicted to the sexual high of murder, and on the night of 14 January he launched his most frantic assault yet. In the space of just fifteen minutes he attacked four students as they slept in their rooms at Florida State University. Straight after the attack he assaulted another FSU student in a separate accommodation block. The resulting carnage was horrific even by Bundy's standards: Lisa Levy was beaten to death, raped and had a nipple bitten off. Margaret Bowman had been severely beaten and then strangled to death. Karen Chandler and Kathy Kleiner survived but suffered broken bones, concussion and severe lacerations. Cheryl Thomas suffered a fractured skull and was left permanently deaf.

Further abduction attempts followed but were thwarted until he targeted 12-year-old Kimberly Diane Leach in Lake City. Her partially mummified remains were found in a shed seven weeks later. By that time, perhaps inevitably, Bundy had been re-arrested. Once again he had driven a stolen car

Twelve-year-old Kimberly Leach, one of Ted Bundy's victims.

erratically straight past a police patrol car, and was pulled over. After a brief struggle, Bundy was subdued and taken to Miami to stand trial on multiple counts of murder. This time there would be no escape. Though Bundy briefly revelled in his centre-stage role representing himself in the trial, he was found guilty and given the death sentence on 24 July 1979. He had previously refused a plea bargain that would have seen him avoid the electric chair: in the end, his ego simply wouldn't allow him to stand before the public and admit his guilt.

Sentenced to death

Further trials followed, and in the end Bundy was given three death sentences for the crimes he committed. While awaiting execution on death row, he gave several interviews and seemed to enjoy the interest in his psychological make-up. He often spoke about himself in the third person, distancing himself from his own past. He spoke of the delight he felt at owning stolen possessions, and referred to murder being the ultimate act of theft – the stealing and possession of another person's life. He spoke of how he would often return to rape the corpses of his victims again and again until their putrefaction prevented any further abuse. He also revealed that he returned to the University of Washington campus to retrieve a pair of earrings and a shoe belonging to Georgann Hawkins the morning after he killed her. To do so, he brazenly strolled through the scores of police officers who were scouring the site for clues. None but a psychopath would have the nerve to do such a thing.

Nobody knows how many Bundy killed in total – he enjoyed lying about his crimes and withholding information about where the bodies might rest. At one point he confessed the total was at least 30, but it could be higher still. Ted Bundy was executed at 7.16 a.m. on 24 January 1989 at Raiford Prison, Florida. He showed no remorse for any of his crimes: 'I guess I am in the enviable position of not having to deal with guilt,' he told one of his interviewers.

INDEX